The Organic Composting Handbook

FEB 2015

The Organic Composting Handbook

Techniques for a Healthy,
Abundant Garden

DEDE CUMMINGS

Foreword by Cheryl Wilfong

Skyhorse Publishing

Skyhorse Publishing books may be purchased in bulk
at special discounts for sales promotion, corporate
gifts, fund-raising, or educational purposes. Special
editions can also be created to specifications.
For details, contact the Special Sales Department,
Skyhorse Publishing, 307 West 36th Street, 11th Floor,
New York, NY 10018 or info@skyhorsepublishing.com.

Skyhorse® and Skyhorse Publishing® are registered
trademarks of Skyhorse Publishing, Inc.®, a Delaware
corporation.

Visit our website at www.skyhorsepublishing.com.

10 9 8 7 6 5 4 3 2 1

Library of Congress Cataloging-in-Publication Data is
available on file.

Cover photo credit: Thinkstock

Print ISBN: 978-1-62914-172-5
Ebook ISBN: 978-1-62914-260-9

Printed in China

CONTENTS

FOREWORD

by Cheryl Wilfong

We know intuitively that organic compost is good for us, good for our garden, and good for our planet. We can join the green planet movement without moving any farther than our own backyards!

We begin simply with our very own organic compost: rich, dark brown, crumbly humus for our houseplants or our flowerbeds. Good enough for our plants to eat. Whether we use compost in our entire vegetable garden or only for the cherry tomato in a pot on our patio, compost nourishes our plants and produces lettuce or tomatoes, beans or broccoli, which in turn nourish us.

As a master gardener and a master composter, I am often asked my advice on compost. All the answers lie within these pages.

Dede Cummings is an author committed to making the world a better place, and this book is an example of her leadership in conservation and in trying to make a difference.

Reading this book, you will have the opportunity to stroll with Dede and her friends through the ins and outs of organic composting. The choice is yours: turn your kitchen waste into a wealth of compost you can use in your garden or waste those nutrients by throwing them in the trash and hauling it to the landfill. Much better of course is filling your own land with the same nutritious food you and your family eat and turning your compost into a haul of treasure. It's as easy as feeding your family, and then feeding the leftovers—your own compostable waste—to your garden.

Another great thing about going, growing, and gardening "green" is that we can save some greenbacks in our wallet by supplying our garden with the rich fertilizer of compost.

Composting ties us into the web of life. We pitch our dead plants onto the pile, and the following spring, new life springs up. Compost is a miracle. Our garden is a miracle, and our planet, well, it's a miracle too. Now, let's start growing our own green miracles with organic compost.

—Cheryl Wilfong, author of *The Meditative Gardener:*
Cultivating Mindfulness of Body, Feelings, and Mind

The author's neighbor down the road in Vermont has a perfectly good compost system made with palettes, and it even works well in winter.

INTRODUCTION

"It must be this voice that is telling me to do something . . . to be concerned about the fate of the world, the fate of this planet."

—Wangari Maathai, Nobel Peace Prize winner, founder of the Green Belt movement in Kenya

I opened up the top of the black plastic bin that always looked to me like Darth Vader sitting silently in my backyard. I imagined it quietly waiting, breathing that same breath from the movie—that scary, wheezing, asthmatic sound that came from under

his mask. Really it was just the compost container I purchased at the town dump for $36 about thirteen years ago.

I remember that when I bought it I had no idea what I was doing. I set it up in about five minutes in the backyard as my children hung around and watched. The little one had his hand on my shoulder and occasionally patted my back and said, "Good work, Mommy!"

It *was* good work when I thought about it. At its very essence, compost is a key ingredient in organic farming because it is made up of organic matter that has been decomposed and recycled as fertilizer and soil amendment. I was creating new and vibrant life while recycling at the same time. In my mind, there was nothing better.

I followed the instructions, setting the thing up on the edge of the yard, slightly in the bushes to keep the black plastic from view, with just enough sun to beat down on it and heat it up. That's the whole idea isn't it? To heat up the compostable matter, give it some air, and turn it occasionally and . . . voilà! You will have rich black soil in a matter of weeks, or a year, depending on how quickly you want to use it.

I really had no clue about composting, so I just started throwing in vegetable scraps and occasional grass clippings from my hand-operated lawnmower.

I used a small plastic bucket that I placed on my kitchen counter by the sink, and any time I ate an apple or a banana or chopped vegetables, I put the peels and cores or other scraps in there.

When it was full and starting to smell, and fruit flies began to gather around it when I opened the lid, I would take it outside, lift the lid of the plastic container, and unceremoniously dump it in the composter.

The beauty of my completely unscientific and carefree system is that it got me excited and interested in composting. The next year, I kept adding to the compost. Once I even used a shovel and turned over the heavy, thick, oozing material, getting a great workout in the process. I realized, however, that I wanted to know how and why it was working, and I began to do research and volunteer for our "cow composting project" in the town where I live. I read about layering the pile, adding twigs and straw, manure, water, and turning. The little black "Darth Vader" was my introduction, and this book is the fruit of the knowledge gained. I want to spread this message, and the book is a way to get more people involved.

The spring after my first composting experiment began, I decided to try using the soil at the bottom of the compost bin to fertilize my flower garden.

It was a Saturday morning, and the kids were still sleeping. I got up, made a cup of tea, and stared outside my kitchen window. There I saw the Darth Vader contraption lurking in the bushes, as if to taunt me, or dare me to come out there and see what lay at the bottom of the pile.

I had never noticed these words before. Oh well, I thought, better late than never.

I approached the black plastic cylinder cautiously. The top lid I noticed had words on it that said, "vent, hi, and low."

I turned the lid so that the arrows lined up, and lifted it off. I peered in cautiously. Always fearful of some critter—perhaps a snake lying there in wait—

I definitely had a respectful relationship with my composter.

When I lifted the lid, I saw that the bin was about three-quarters full, and looked like a gigantic science experiment, with worms and bugs crawling, flies buzzing around, and smells that rose up with the steam.

I stood staring down at my compost pile in wonderment. I felt as if I had created a great work of art. I was quiet, meditating on the power of decay. I realized how connected we are: what we grow, what we eat, and what we throw away is somehow all tied together. It was a powerful moment, and I recall feeling very small, yet at the same time, a part of a great mystery.

I had my wheelbarrow with me, the one that has the slow leak in the tire so that I have to pump it full of air before every use (I'm too lazy to patch it). I bent over and slid open the small rectangular panel on the lower half of the composter. I felt a tingling of excitement as I watched the rich earth tumble out of the lower half of the panel. I began to shovel the dirt into my wheelbarrow, feeling the amazement of having created something I would pay a lot of money for at the garden center!

I began walking around my flower gardens, from bed to bed, dumping shovelfuls of this rich earth around the base of the flowers. As soon as the three kids woke up, I dragged them outside to look at what I had accomplished—no, what we as a family had accomplished!

Much to my chagrin, they were not impressed at all—they yawned and went back into the house to play video games and watch Saturday morning cartoons.

I stood outside in my backyard, with my hands on my hips, surveying the flowerbeds. The rich earth glowed in the early morning sunlight, and, to my mind, the plants looked healthier already.

Through the magic of my composting, the flowers were taking in the rich nitrogen from the new soil through their roots, absorbing it with the old soil and making it all richer. I was increasing the yield and production of my flower beds and this was a memorable moment. I knew I was hooked—as a gardener and now, an avid composter. It isn't that hard to do, and if I can do it, so can you. I hope this book will inspire you, whether you live on a farm or a rural area, in the suburbs, or in a city.

Don't put it off. Start now and you will be amazed at the results. It doesn't take a lot of money, or time, and I will show you how.

The benefits of composting are manifest in the peace of mind you feel when you know you are cutting down on the waste stream to landfills, saving money, and improving the horticulture where you live.

The Organic Composting Handbook

Chapter 1

WHAT IS COMPOSTING?

"In the spring, at the end of the day, you should smell like dirt."

—Margaret Atwood, *Bluebeard's Egg*

When you go for a walk, whether it's in the woods or along a public trail in mid-city, the surrounding ground appears in your peripheral vision. You see leaves pile up in the fall, swirling about you as they fall from the trees, and wedging themselves among broken-down tree limbs that are scattered about. All this will decay and become part of a timeless system of breakdown and rebirth. But the system is not for the impatient. The process takes a thousand years or so just to make about an inch of composted soil.

You don't have a thousand years, though, so I'm here to tell you how to speed up this natural process while yielding similar results. This book is meant to be a guide, sometimes humorous, but always with the goal of respect for the planet Earth and all its inhabitants.

What is composting?

First things first. Of course, I will go into much great detail later, but as we start here, a simple explanation:

The view from the author's land of an adjoining farmer's hayfield, left, and her tools for a spring garden, above.

Composting is the decomposition of organic matter into a nutrient-rich soil amendment. Finished compost is an earthy humus-rich material that helps soil retain nutrients and moisture to improve plant growth.

Anything that can decompose is biodegradable material. Biodegradable materials include wood chips, twigs, straw, paper, leaves, manure, fruits, and vegetables. Some less common materials are dryer lint, kelp, junk mail, and old cotton clothes. All of these materials can be composted at home.

Why should I compost?

Food scraps make up one third of a typical household's trash. When food scraps are sent to the landfill, they take up limited space and contribute to increased production of methane and toxic leachate. According to Highfields, a center for composting research and education, if all the food scraps in Vermont—where I live and compost—were composted instead of being sent to the landfill, it would offset the same amount of carbon as not burning twelve million gallons of gasoline a year! By composting organic waste, we close the loop on our food system. The valuable nutrients in our food scraps are used to regenerate soil and grow more food.

The author adding a thin layer of compost to one of her raised beds in the fall.

Before You Begin: A Few Tips

As we begin the process of learning how to compost, it is important to remember and understand that *compost is not a fertilizer!* Although it contains many plant-available nutrients, compost is primarily a soil-conditioning amendment.

Apply compost when you are preparing your garden soil in the spring, or when you are putting your garden to bed in the fall. Compost is typically applied to gardens annually—a thin layer (1/2"–2" thick) can be spread on the garden and worked into the soil.

The author's garden "put to bed" in the fall.

For potted plants, mix compost into your potting media at roughly 25 percent by volume. For seasonal maintenance, "top-dress" potted plants with a thin layer of compost.

Testing our soil for nutrient deficiencies and our compost for nutrient content will give you more precise information about how to improve your specific soil conditions. Using compost together with cover crops and organic fertilizers is a sustainable way to maintain your soil's fertility.

By taking the first step to begin composting your food scraps and your garden debris, you are on your way to reaping the finished product, which is a mixture of decomposed organic matter rich in nutrients and perfect for adding back to your own garden soil or donating to a community garden.

HOW TO USE A BLACK PLASTIC COMPOSTER

A black plastic composter is a good way to get started composting. Then once you have your composting routine established, you'll better know your needs and be able to customize your personal compost system.

Black plastic compost bins and tumblers are great for collecting and containing kitchen scraps, and they are good at keeping smells and critters away, to some extent, but they're not so good at producing finished compost. The types of things you can put in them are limited.

A black plastic composter is a finicky eater. It is built to digest kitchen scraps with some dead leaves or maybe a bit of hay for balance. Throw in a shovelful of dirt occasionally to add micro-organisms.

Since the diet of a black plastic composter is somewhat restricted, you can collect many of the things you would otherwise throw into a compost bin and take them to the composting program at your landfill: paper napkins, paper towels, and pizza boxes. Because orange peels and grapefruit rinds and eggshells take a long time to decompose in a composter, you can also take those.

You can dig a few trowelfuls of compost out of the bottom, but then you run the risk of the garbage inside collapsing into the space you've created, and that's the end of your compost collection.

The tumblers can be heavy to turn and thus become an unwanted chore.

Some persistent critters do try to burrow into the composter from the bottom. And it will take less than a week for raccoons to figure out how to take off the lid, if there is one. Dogs will also tear off the lid.

If you outgrow your composter, you can use it as a storage bin rather than for actual composting. You can store your raw garbage in the composter during the winter when very little composting is actually happening. Or you can store your finished compost in the composter so the nutrients won't leach out.

A black plastic composter looks neat, contains smells, and gives the illusion of keeping critters out. Those benefits are a definite perk for anyone new to composting. —Cheryl Wilfong

The author's fancy new composter—see directions on page 35.

Composting is really quite simple.

To activate the billions of microbes that are alive and thriving in such things as food scraps and garden waste and a vital part part of the process of decomposition, build them a structure in which they can creep and crawl into your compost pile. Inside the structure will be not only the food scraps and garden wastes, but also brown debris, like leaves and sticks. Just make sure that there's plenty of air and moisture in the pile. Sounds simple, right? It really is.

In this book, you'll hear the voices of other composters, most notably master composter and author of *The Meditative Gardener*, Cheryl Wilfong, who happens to be a neighbor. Since everyone

is different, and people move at their own pace, there isn't any fast and fixed rule how, what, or where to compost. In the sidebar below, there is even a story about a woman who just puts everything in a pile wrapped simply with chicken wire, and she creates the best "leaf mold" this way. She never touches it until she needs it to mix it into her garden as a soil conditioner.

LEAF MOLD

Leaf mold is good for your soil.

Our local garden columnist, Henry Homeyer, wrote about leaf mold as a soil conditioner a few years ago, so I thought I'd try it. I made a cylinder of chicken wire, about four or five feet in diameter, and I staked it into the ground with some old broom handles and a couple of stray fence posts I happened to have. I cut the chicken wire so that I simply bent and hooked the end wires onto the beginning mesh.

That fall I filled the wired cylinder to the brim with leaves from the yard. Then I forgot about it for two years.

I recently looked at it, and, oh my, that humus is dark and beautiful. Four feet of leaves settled down into six inches of leaf mold.

If you pay more attention to your leaves than I did, the leaves will decompose faster if they are wet. Watering them once a week prevents them from drying out and thereby slowing down the decomposition process.

If you feel energetic, you can line your enclosure with cardboard, which will help maintain dampness. And if you feel really energetic, you can shred the leaves with the lawn mower before dumping them into the wire cage. That way you can fit more in. Or, build a bin out of four pallets, and fill it with leaves. A pallet bin and a four-foot wide chicken-wire cylinder will both hold about sixteen trash bags of leaves.

If you leave the pile high and dry, it will take two years to mold. This mold is an excellent soil amendment that offer good water retention qualities along with additional nutrients. It helps to increase soil structure and aids soil fertility. —Cheryl Wilfong

Workers at Vermont Compost harvesting potatoes on the farm.

Chapter 2

WHY IS COMPOSTING IMPORTANT?

"What you do every day is what forms your mind and precious few of us can or would spend most days outdoors."

—Bill McKibben, 350.org leader and renowned environmentalist

The Good That Will Come Out of It

Once you decide to begin composting, you will begin to nurture and improve your home environment. You are preserving the Earth, and making your landfill load much lighter—maybe even eliminating it altogether! You will have fewer runs to the dump, and more money to spend on beautiful shrubs or supplies from the garden center.

It's Natural
Composting works with nature by using recycled yard waste and kitchen scraps and breaking them down using microorganisms and earthworms.

Good for the Soil
Composting will return beneficial nutrients like nitrogen potassium, phosphorus, and many other minerals back into the soil to be released over a few years to improve the overall health of the plants or garden.

Good for the Spirit

In this book, I emphasize that composting is also a way to increase one's "happiness quotient." By composting you are improving the natural environment where you live, and you may gain some friends in the process: like neighbors, for instance, who might be curious about what you are doing, or your fellow community gardeners, who might want to share ideas which may lead to, well, friendship.

THE MORE BINS, THE BETTER

What's the best method of composting? It depends where you live.

If you live in an urban area or even a busy and tightly-packed town where your outdoor space is limited, you will want a smaller black plastic unit. They are fairly easy to find. Our landfill sells them cheaper than you can buy them from catalogs. Consider buying two so you can add to one while the other is "resting." It is difficult to get at the compost while the unit is still "working." Otherwise, you suffer the frustration of trying to ladle out a trowelful of compost from the underside of a digesting black plastic belly.

If you live in bear country, you'll need a really big, heavy, black plastic unit that the lid screws onto. The bears may roll it away, but they (hopefully) won't be able to get into it.

I live in the country and have plenty of room, so I have three open bins—each made of four pallets set in a square and simply tied together with rope at each corner. Very easy and uncomplicated. You can build one in ten minutes and take it apart in five. I live near a company that uses a lot of paper products and is always giving away pallets. A local company (that uses a lot of paper products) always has a pile of pallets to give away. Once a year, I drive my truck over there and load up.

I line up the three bins beside each other—one I am "adding to"; one is resting; and one I am "subtracting from," using the cooked compost for planting or to scatter on various garden beds.

I add to the newest one every day—garbage and leaves, flower deadheads, and garden trimmings. The middle-aged pile was topped off last fall with a layer of manure from the local farm. It just sits there, resting and gestating, lost under an accumulation of last fall's leaves.

The third pile—the one that I'm subtracting from—collected a winter's cap of leaves to keep itself warm, but in the spring, I rake it clean and toss the leaves into the neighboring "add to" bin. Having removed the skim of leaves, I finally see the sunken heap, only half as high as it was in the fall—this is composting at work. Dead leaves, dead mums, dead flowers, and garbage have all been miraculously digested and transformed into living soil. This pile is the one I dig into almost every day—using its rich black humus to transplant plants or to pot up extra plants I find volunteering in places I don't want them.

When the "subtract from" bin is totally empty, the pallets that surrounded have become quite decrepit. After two or three years of holding compost, the pallets themselves have also rotted. I haul them off to a brush pile and erect new pallets. The now empty bin becomes the new "add to" pile, the old "resting" heap becomes the "subtract from" pile, and the former "add to" agglomeration can now "rest."

All this adding to and subtracting from "adds up" to beautiful compost for the garden. —Cheryl Wilfong

A Great Way to Save Money

Composting will decrease the amount of household waste sent to the landfill, as much as thirty-five percent in some cases! The fact that there will be less garbage to send out will save money all around. You'll also see lower water bills when the compost eventually becomes excellent mulch for the garden, because more moisture will be retained. It appears that this form of recycling is a win-win situation!

Last but Not Least

As I mentioned composting will conserve water, but once it's used it will also protect the plants by covering up their roots from exposure and when it's mixed into the soil, it will add drainage and create more beneficial places in which to plant. It will reduce the risk of soil disease as well and help keep weeds from growing in your garden.

Closing the Loop

The mission of Highfields Center for Composting, in Vermont was "to close the loop on community-based, sustainable food and agricultural systems, thus addressing soil health, water quality, solid waste, farm viability, and climate change."

According to Highfields founder Tom Gilbert, composting has been around for thousands of years.

Bacteria have been breaking down organic materials for billions of years, but the credit for discovering compost may go to the settlers of the Fertile Crescent over ten thousand years ago. They noticed that plants grew better when they were next to manure and soon started spreading manure on their crops. Native Americans were hip to the benefits of compost and taught the first New Englanders their recipe—ten parts muck to one fish, turn periodically until the fish disintegrates.

In the early part of the twentieth century, chemical fertilizers were used for agricultural purposes and proved to be so successful very few people believed there could be anything bad about them. Chemical fertilizers are the bane of most organic farmers and gardeners. Not only have they been proven to trickle down into rivers via runoff from farmland, they ultimately kill the soil even in the backyard garden.

Purchasing a fertilizer that is labeled as "organic" can be misleading—many of these so-called fertilizers are harmful.

However, back in the early twentieth century, on many farms, especially in places like Vermont with an agrarian society, the old-fashioned composting techniques were still being used—they were just somewhat dormant.

Nowadays farming has gone back to traditional methods of using manure as compost, rotating crops, and cycling through organic soil preparations that restore balance and increase productivity. A biodynamic approach to farming with compost preparations was first introduced by Rudolf Steiner around 1924 and is a fermenting practice involving herbs that is still being used today.

Benefits of Composting

Compost can significantly improve soil quality and protect the environment in a number of ways:
- Improves soil structure
- Increases nutrient content in soil
- Improves moisture retention
- Increases soil aeration
- Remediates contaminated soil

- Reduces plant diseases and pests and thus reduces need for pesticides and fungicides
- Reduces or eliminates need for chemical fertilizers
- Improves organic matter and carbon in soils
- Reduces storm-water runoff and soil erosion
- Feeds the soil-to-food cycle of sustainability and keeps soil and plants pesticide-free

For information and tools, see the Recources section on Highfields Center for Composting (highfieldscomposting.org).

The benefits of using compost to enrich soil are myriad. The bottom line is that composting creates rich and nutritious soil that will be aerated and not subject to as much erosion. The newly composted soil, when mixed into garden beds at the beginning of the season, will create a home for earthworms, micro-organisms, and bacteria that will ultimately protect plants against disease.

Generally speaking, the decomposition process involves both:

Aerobic: oxygen decomposes and stabilizes the composting materials.

Anaerobic: a lack of oxygen breaks down composition by the actions of living organisms.

The dual process of aerobic and anaerobic decomposition balances wet/dry conditions in the pile and creates an atmosphere most suited to attracting the best organisms for the job. Organisms like fungi, mold, and bacteria literally feed upon this decaying vegetation of the compost pile. Later in the process, other organisms come into the "kingdom" of the compost pile: critters like earthworms and centipedes (I must admit, not my favorite creatures) further break down and enrich the compost.

GOOD COMPOST TAKES TIME

My neighbor complains that her compost pile barely produces any compost. She piles up all the brown stuff in the fall, and in the spring, it's still brown. After forty-five minutes of sorting through all the phlox stems and squash vines from last year, she finally finds some compost—just enough to fill a wheelbarrow.

"Your compost looks so great," she tells me. "How do you do it?"

"Time" is my answer. The soil in my compost bin is rich and dark, there's plenty of it, and it's three years old. I build a compost pile and leave it alone for two or three years. I do not pull it apart the following spring. I am not tempted to just throw a handful of compost on top of an old bin.

To help my patience and my composting, I use three compost bins: one for this year, a second from the last year, and a third from the year before that. The bin I'm taking rich, dark compost from now now was put together three years ago; I know this because I just found the not-yet-decomposed bamboo paper plates from a neighbor's daughter's outdoor wedding three summers ago. I pitched those flimsy remains into the current "new" bin to which I'm adding. Maybe they'll finally be biodegraded the next time I see them, three years from now.

I am as busy in my life as the next person. I do not have the time, energy, or desire to turn a compost pile, and neither do you. So, instead of using your precious time for the care and feeding and turning of the compost pile, don't give yourself a hard time about your pathetic compost pile. Just let Nature take her time and do the work of composting for you. —Cheryl Wilfong

THE COLORS OF COMPOST

An active compost pile has a mixture of high nitrogen, moist materials called "greens," and drier, carbon-rich materials called "browns." (For a more detailed list of green and brown material, turn to Compost Alphabet on page 28 in Chapter Three.) There is nothing better to add to your soil, and the folks at Highfields describe it in their educational material as follows:

GREENS INCLUDE: Food scraps (such as fruit and vegetable peels, coffee grounds, tea bags, and pre-pared foods), fresh grass clippings, fresh weeds and manures. "Green" refers not to color but to composting potential.

BROWNS INCLUDE: Dry weeds, straw, fallen leaves, shredded paper, sawdust, and wood chips.

BENEFITS FOR THE SOIL

All our food—including animal products and processed—originates from the Earth, according to the "Teachers' Guide to Compost Activities: Do the Rot Thing," a pamphlet published by the Alameda County Waste Management Authority & Source Reduction and Recycling Board in San Leandro, California with contributions from Highfields. We trace our food back to its original form, and from there back to the soil, which illustrates the importance of healthy soil. When we send our biodegradable materials to the landfill, we waste valuable nutrients that our soil needs to give new life. Through composting, we recycle our biodegradable materials and give them back to the soil. Compost feeds the billions of soil organisms that are essential in healthy soil. Healthy soil means healthy plants, which means healthy people and animals.

Source: Composting Across the Curriculum, Marin County Department of Solid Waste

Benefits for Plants

Without decomposers such as bacteria, fungi, worms, ants, beetles, and mites, decomposition would stop and resources that sustain life would be depleted. A seemingly endless variety of decomposers all serve different functions in the decomposition process.

As compost breaks down in the soil, it provides the fertilizing nutrients of nitrogen, phosphorus, and potassium in forms that are readily available to plants. Unlike most inorganic fertilizers, compost functions as a slow-release store of nutrients, so that the nutrients are available as the plants require them instead of in one intense flush. Compost also provides a wide range of important micronutrients not found in commercial fertilizers.

Added to sandy soils, the organic matter in compost increases the soil's water-holding ability so that both rain and irrigation

A cosmos flower from the author's garden.

An organic vegetable garden with improved soil structure.

water are held in the root zone for plant use. This can significantly lower the irrigation requirements in the orchard industry and other applications where water use is restricted or prohibitively expensive. Compost lightens heavy (high clay) soils, allowing better infiltration of both air and water into the root zone. This improves plant health and helps to prevent sealing of the soil surface caused by water pooling. Organic matter functions like a sponge, enabling soil to retain nutrients and moisture in the root zone. Inorganic fertilizer nutrients as well as those released by the compost itself are kept from leaching down into ground water. Soil structure is improved, allowing effective drainage, extensive root growth, and soil aggregate stabilization, so that soil is less subject to erosion by either water or wind. Earthworm activity is encouraged, further enhancing soil fertility.

Benefits for People

In their "Guide to Home Composting," the folks at Highfields begin with this helpful paragraph:

"Remember that every compost pile is unique. It may take time to create the right recipe for proper decomposition, so be patent and have fun!"

You can help your children learn about the benefits of composting by asking them to look through their lunches and think of ways to reduce the amount of garbage— this simple activity helps them find their own way of helping the earth. Children will also have the opportunity to learn what natural resources were consumed to make this waste. Other benefits include:

Less Smelly Trash—Reduces Odor Problems
Many new composting individuals, families, schools or businesses find that composting drastically reduces odor problems associated with their trash.

Reduce Trash Collection Costs
By weight, food scraps can be 50 percent or more of a food service business's waste stream. Participating in a composting program reduces the weight of your trash, which could result in reduction in your trash disposal costs.

Introduce the Reduce, Reuse, Recycle Hierarchy
Reducing the amount of packaging is best. Reusing a package is second best. Recycling/composting comes in third, with landfilling as a last resort.

The author's containers for reducing the amount of packaging. At local food coops, and many supermarkets with bulk buying options, you can bring your own containers to fill up, thereby reducing packaging.

Benefits for the Planet

We use materials from the Earth every day for everything we do. We eat food, drink from aluminum cans or glass bottles, live in wooden houses, wear clothing made from cotton or synthetic fibers, and use many plastic appliances. Some of these materials, such as metals and plastics, are non-biodegradable. These materials do not decompose, although many of them can be recycled.

Biodegradable materials decay; examples include wood, food scraps, paper, and grass clippings. Anything that is biodegradable can be composted.

The author's containers she uses at home for bulk purchases that save packaging.

A Tangible Way to Go Green
Composting as little as five gallons of food scraps prevents the release of greenhouse gasses equivalent to burning over one gallon of gasoline.

Reduce Your Carbon Footprint
Composting as little as five gallons of food scraps prevents the release of greenhouse gasses equivalent to burning over one gallon of gasoline.

Students at Cambridge (Vermont) Elementary School composting their food scraps.

We Are What We Eat

Once when my children were little, I looked out the kitchen window to see my daughter, Emma, then probably four, out in our garden on her hands and knees eating beans from the garden right off the vine.

"Emma! You really need to bring those beans inside so I can wash them and then you can eat them."

"Why?" she asked, clearly perplexed.

Well, I didn't really know why. Since I wasn't using any chemical fertilizers or pesticides, there wasn't anything I could think of that might harm her. If she accidentally ate a bit of soil, at least it would be clean. So, I let her stay out there in the garden and eat the raw vegetables right from the vine. How wonderful to feel confident that the food we were producing was perfectly safe and healthy!

A tomato plant with morning glories in full bloom in the author's garden.

THE BOTTOM OF THE COMPOST PILE

Yes, I know you're not supposed to put animal products in a compost pile, and most composters agree not to put animal waste or dairy in the pile, but sometimes Vermonter Cheryl Wilfong does it anyway:

I come to the bottom of one compost pile in early May. I love the excavation, perhaps because I wanted to be an archaeologist when I was eleven.

I find desiccated chicken bones. Nowadays I cremate bones and bacon grease in my wood stove before I add them to the pile.

In addition to the chicken bones, I find the bamboo plates from my neighbors' daughter's wedding, now three years old, and rib bones the from barbeque place that catered it. While the bamboo plates are biodegradable, they're still completely recognizable. The plastic cups made from corn have now splintered. And if I opt to throw them in the trash I'm not counting on their biodegradability.

I wheelbarrow loads of compost to the vegetable garden and sprinkle bucketfuls on my former herb garden that I'm refurbishing as a flower-vegetable medley garden.

I pot up my extra plants. Really, this is the main reason I garden: so that I can give plants away.

I pot up plants for the Perennial Swappers that meet every two weeks, for the Brattleboro Garden Club plant sale on Memorial Day weekend, and for the Putney Library plant sale in early June. Every Saturday morning, I scavenge free flowerpots at the Swap Shop at the landfill. I recycle every yogurt container, hummus container, and take-out box, and reuse them for potting up little plants.

Now I'm digging up and dividing the biggest clumps of gone-by daffodils. These require medium-size pots and several handfuls of compost in each one. As I paw through the compost, I toss the desiccated bones into the woods behind the compost bins. After a number of years, the soil around the bins becomes quite dark and rich too.

When I reach the bottom of the compost pile, I drive the truck to Mail-Rite to pick up some new pallets and reconstruct the old bins whose pallet sides look like decayed teeth. I tie the new pallets together at the corners and lay down a black plastic floor to prevent tree roots from sucking up the compost from the bottom.

Then I toss in the latest offerings: dead daffodils and coffee grounds still in their brown paper filter, orange and grapefruit rinds, banana peels, and, well, I can't help myself, a few fish bones. —Cheryl Wilfong

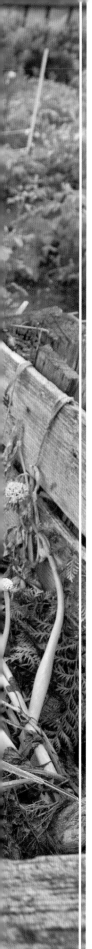

Chapter 3

COMPOSTING 101

"If you have a garden and a library, you have everything you need."

—Cicero

Composting is a biological process that breaks down organic waste and turns that into humus that has the same look and feel as ordinary dirt.

But it is far from ordinary. Compost is the end result of a complex process that involves worms and insects, fungi and bacteria, and it leads to this organic material being broken down slowly in a pile in your backyard or as quickly as you start collecting in a container under your sink.

HIDDEN IN PLAIN VIEW

Your compost pile must be handy and easy to get to, otherwise, you won't go there. If you want to actually use your compost bin, put it close to a path you regularly travel. In other words, hide it in plain view.

My driveway is bordered by trees and shrubs. I put my three compost bins in a parking area is off to the left, hiding behind a forsythia bush. I usually park my car in front of the bins.

When visitors turn into the driveway, they see the house with eye-popping magenta trim. They see an arbor beckoning them into the garden beyond. The corner of their eye may register a green bush and a blue car, but not the compost bins that are ten feet from where they park.

These focal points of house, arbor, and garden distract the visitor's eye. They are not seeing what's on the left side of the driveway. Many people don't even see that there's a parking area for their car, right beside my car! Instead they park in front of the garage door.

When they get out of their car, they are looking at the gardens or the front door, and not at those camouflaged compost bins behind them. In the summer, I further disguise the bins with morning glories growing over the compost bin fencing.

You also want your compost bin to be accessible in winter. For those of us in the North Country, this means placing it within a few, and I mean a very few, feet of your snowplowed driveway. You don't want to wade through knee-deep snow and have to snowshoe over there. Nor do you want to have to shovel a path through three feet of snow. My compost pile is eighteen inches from the driveway. In the winter, that's a mere two shovelfuls of snow.

Every day, when I walk out to my car, my sweetie reminds me to take out the little kitchen bucket full of compost. Maybe that compost pile is too handy? —Cheryl Wilfong

WINTER COMPOSTING

If you're not keen on trudging out to the winter compost pile, then you can accumulate more compost before you trek out to the deep freezer of the great outdoors.

My compost bucket holds less than two quarts, so I have to walk to my compost pile at least once and usually twice a day. Fortunately, my compost pile is inches away from my driveway, so I have easy access, even in deep snow.

My neighbors keep a step-on trashcan under their sink. Although this is very convenient, I do sometimes suspect the smell in their house emanates from their three-gallon collection of kitchen scraps.

Ben keeps a five-gallon bucket on his unheated back porch and collects his compost there. Then once a month, when the weather is good, he trudges out to his compost heap in the backyard. Yes, the compost is probably frozen into the bucket, but he simply turns the bucket upside down on the compost heap, and gives it a few good thwacks with a shovel until the giant compost ice cube falls out.

The author's trek to her compost bin in winter . . . and what she finds there.

Barbara, who lives in town, keeps her compost in a small box in her car in the winter. Most nights, it freezes solid. Then, when she happens to be driving by the landfill, she can deliver her frozen dinner leftovers to the composting program.

How close is your winter compost? Too close (in the kitchen)? Too far away (through the snowy yard or on the other side of town)? Or just right (beside the driveway)?

How often you need to go depends on whether you can hold it. But then, when you've gotta go, you've gotta go. —Cheryl Wilfong

The author emptying her kitchen compost bucket.

Decomposers turn our garbage into plant food.

There are many different animals that help break down organic materials into the rich soil helper we know as compost. A compost pile and worm bin has an entire network of different bugs. Bacteria do most of the work, even though they are invisible to the naked eye. Other animals large enough to see, such as beetles, worms, centipedes, millipedes, and sow bugs, are also important decomposers. Without decomposer animals, all life would stop because new plants would not have the necessary nutrients needed to grow.

Foodscraps at Highfields.

The composting cycle works as follows:
The carbon/nitrogen ratio—

The material that comes into the compost is referred to as "green material," and can include fresh vegetable debris, like stems and stalks you don't want to eat, and grass clippings. You can also add brown material to your compost pile, like dried leaves. To create an optimal carbon/nitrogen ratio—which is a crucial balancing act, throw in two parts brown material to one part green material.

RECYCLED COMPOST BINS

My friend, Mary Lou, recycles whatever she has on hand rather than going out and buying something new.[1] Her husband is a contractor, so she constructed her compost bins out of cement blocks held in place with metal fence posts in every other block to prevent them from collapsing.

She divided her ten-foot-long U-shaped bin into three sections by salvaging some corrugated translucent fiberglass roofing panels left over from a cold frame. Sections of metal roofing work just as well. The panels are held in place by more metal fence posts.

Here's how Mary Lou's three-bin system works:

She adds to the bin on the left. The middle bin "rests." The bin on the right is "finished." When the "finished" bin is empty or when the first "receiving" bin is full, whichever comes first, she forks the middle bin into the third, then forks the first into the middle.

Mary Lou has a big house and a small yard in town. Her upstairs tenant and a couple of friends contribute their kitchen scraps to her compost bin too. Mary Lou not only recycles found materials, she also recycles her friends' materials. —Cheryl Wilfong

---

1 Freecycle.org is an excellent way to find free materials near you. Join your city or regional freecycle and post your requests for whatever you have to give away or whatever materials you might be searching for.

Temperature—

Heat is important to accelerate the compost process. The best temperature for your compost is between 90 and 135°F (30–60°C). The composting process will slow down when the temperature falls below this range.

The author recommends chopping up hard to breakdown fruits and veggies like this melon in order to accelerate the process once the food scraps get thrown in the pile.

Oxygenation—

Oxygen is crucial for all inhabitants within the compost pile, including microbes, which decompose at a much faster rate than anaerobic waste material. Proper ventilation is achieved through turning the compost pile and making sure that it is here rated in the next pile may take three to four times longer to create beneficial humus.

Smaller Waste Products—

Chopping up your green kitchen scaps into smaller pieces can really speed up the composting process is chopping up your kitchen green scraps into smaller pieces. You can shred and chip brown garden clippings and make them smaller, too.

Water—

If the compost pile is too dry, it will decompose very slowly. During dry spells, it is necessary to add a little water to the compost to help speed up the process. However, if it is too wet, the, process can begin to create a foul odor and the density will create compression that isn't conducive to proper balance of the carbon-nitrogen ratio.

What to Put into Your Compost

All greens that are nitrogen-rich, such as vegetable and fruit scraps, eggshells, grass clippings, coffee and tea grounds, and (non-toxic) flowers or plants are safe to put into your compost pile.

You can also compost brown material, like dry leaves or wood chips, hay, or small twigs. Newspapers and paper can be added if they are crumpled or ripped into small pieces, but it's better to recycle them if you can.

What Not to Put in Your Compost

Meat, bones, fish, cheese, or other dairy products, pet or human waste, metal or plastic, any fat (like buttered bread), or diseased plants or weeds. It's very important not to put weeds in your compost because the weeds will come back into your garden.

DANCING RACCOONS

At my annual month-long meditation retreat, my daily chore was to take out the trash, the compost, and the recycling. What a perfect job for this master composter!

As I walked out the kitchen door with a five-gallon bucket of kitchen waste, I would sometimes be met by a dancing raccoon torn between wanting the contents of the bucket and being too shy to come close. Wanting and not wanting. How many times a day is this same civil war re-enacted in our own minds? he raccoons want the pleasant (garbage in a bucket), and don't want the unpleasant (People! People!). We want the pleasant (beautiful compost), but not the unpleasant (raccoons!).

This ongoing dance of attraction and repulsion is one definition of stress. We, like the raccoons, want to approach the goodies, but we also want to avoid some unpleasantness or other. We build our compost pile, and then it doesn't look as good as we wanted. We want beautiful compost, but what we get is gush with dried stems. We want a garden that looks like the one in the magazine and what we have is a weed patch.

This is the dance of life: pleasant-unpleasant, want-don't want. Knowing that pleasant and unpleasant are constantly arising and ceasing, we could just dance with life. —Cheryl Wilfong

NOS AND YESSES FOR YOUR COMPOST PILE

No.
Weeds: Do not put any weeds you dig up from your garden or flower beds into the compost because the seeds will spread and come back to haunt you!
Hay: grass, alfalfa, clover, etc. cut and dried for use as fodder. A farmer feeds hay to his cows when fresh green grass isn't available.

Yes.
Straw: hollow stalks of grain after threshing, used for bedding, for weaving hats, baskets, mulch, and more.

Easy Steps to Begin Composting Today:

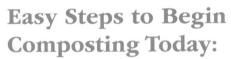

What is Compost?: Compost is alive, stable, aerobic, earthy, dark, cool, and regenerative.

1. Choose Your Bin—Any old receptacle will do, but you want to make sure it is in a sunny spot. Bins come in all shapes and sizes. There is no "right" one to make and/or buy. The pallet bin I talk about in this book came about after years of composting and lots of research—it is a relatively simple thing to make.

2. Add a productive mix of high-in-nitrogen, moist materials called "greens,"(food scraps, such as fruit and vegetable scraps, coffee grounds, tea bags—with staple removed—or tea grounds from tea balls, fresh grass clippings, and manure) and drier, carbon-rich material called "browns (fallen leaves, shredded paper, wood chips, and straw)."

3. Layer by adding the greens and browns alternately. Each time you add food scraps, cover them with brown or with partially degraded materials to deter unwanted creatures from intruding.

4. Let bugs do the work. Fungi and bacteria are microorganisms that do the majority of the work for you in the compost pile.

5. Let the compost breathe by turning, or mixing, the pile approximately two times per month (though some

composters do things differently, or never turn their piles!). Composting organisms need oxygen—adding more air will speed up the process.

6. Keep the pile moist by adding water—if too dry, add leaves or shredded newspaper. One surefire way to test your pile for moisture quality is to take a handful of material from the center of the pile and squeeze it. It should feel like a "wrung-out sponge," according to the folks at Highfields.

CRITTER FEEDER

Yes, critters come to my compost pile. I see chipmunks and bluejays picking their way through it in the morning, and I'm sure raccoons come at night, because someone is licking the eggshells clean.

One May morning, I saw a red squirrel jump out of the compost bin and on to a nearby pine tree with an avocado shell in its mouth. Up the tree it dashed, leaving me with the image of a red squirrel in a sombrero eating guacamole and chittering "Ai-yi-yi-yi."

You could think of your compost pile as a big, perhaps somewhat unsightly, bird or squirrel feeder. Cute. But when it comes to bigger critters, you or your neighbors may express some concern. You really don't want a neighborhood dog pawing through the remains of last night's dinner. And you do not want to attract bears. As to the mid-sized mammals who are happy to dine at the buffet table of the compost pile for their own moonlight dinner, well, that's your decision.

Fear of critters is the number-one reason people decide not to compost. But there are ways around this issue. One is to avoid putting your kitchen waste on the pile. You can still run it through the garbage disposal and send all those nutrients downstream. Or you could bury it eight inches deep in the garden. Another way is to compost indoors using red worms in a Rubbermaid tub.

Your compost is dinner in disguise for someone. Who will that be? —Cheryl Wilfong

Critters in the Compost and the Job They Do

When I turn over my compost pile, or dump shovelfuls into the wheelbarrow, I usually have a moment when I hesitate before sinking in the shovel. Why? I've been composting for some twenty years, and I still hesitate with this tiny, almost imperceptible, sense of fear at what I might find under that shovel!

I decided to get serious, and I began to learn about what was in the pile—this, obviously, will be a great activity for kids! If you have the time and the motivation, you can start a little science experiment in your backyard.

The bacterium in your compost pile is so small you can't even see it. It is everywhere. There's fungus, or mold, like you sometimes see growing on a decaying piece of food in your refrigerator or in your worm bin.

Oh, and the bugs! They are legion and fascinating when you turn your compost pile with a shovel, and it is amazing what you will discover. Though the sight of a centipede always sends horror movie tingles down my spin, I can't stop looking at them, and don't even try to count their legs! Earthworms are my favorite! They don't have eyes or legs and have a soft body that is divided into segments—they just move around sensing the light, but they prefer dark moist places like the compost pile where they eat bacteria and fungi. There are so many more I can't even begin to name, but here are a few to look out for when you bend down low: pill bugs, ants, fruit flies, mites, slugs, snails, and one of my personal favorites, spiders, who help eat insects and control pests that can harm the garden, and build webs that sparkle in the morning dew. How these bugs work in the compost pile could be the subject of another book!

BACKSTAGE IN THE GARDEN

When I visit a garden, I'm always on the lookout for where the gardeners hide their inventory. Every beautiful garden has a back stage, and I want to see it.

Where do they hide the compost? The brush pile? In the heaps of woodchips or bark mulch? Where do they put the dead plants? Do they pot up their divided plants? How do they camouflage the inner workings?

I like this treasure hunt. Where are the tools of the trade located? The shovels, the flowerpots, the clippers and loppers? Where do they keep the stuff that makes the garden beautiful?

The set and the scenery of the garden itself might be something I can only fantasize about, but more than garden gnomes are at work. Real people have been sweating, digging, and hauling, although by the time I arrive, their tracks have been covered, the walks have been swept, and all is calm.

Sometimes, the storage area is beautiful too. (Although that's nearly beyond my personal comprehension.) A few gardeners actually do find a place for everything, and put everything in its place. But, more often, behind the scenes looks not unlike the back staging area of my garden—heaps of unused or disused garden material.

Then I stroll contentedly back into the garden and greet the owner in her clean clothes and clogs. —Cheryl Wilfong

COMPOST ALPHABET —Cheryl Wilfong

Green = Nitrogen
Apple cores
Banana skins
Coffee grounds in filters
Daffodil deadheads
Eggshells
Feathers
Grapefruit skins
Grass clippings
Horseradish leaves
Iceberg lettuce
Juice pulp
Kiwi skins
Lettuce leaves
Manure (herbivores)
Nasturtium leaves
Orange rinds
Pumpkin
Quinoa
Rhubarb leaves
Seaweed (wash off salt)
Teabags
Urine
Vegetables
Watermelon rinds
Ximenia (sourplum)
Xanthorhizus (yellow root)
Yams
Zucchini

**Brown = Carbon
(and Carbohydrates)**
Agave syrup (sugar)
Brown paper bags
Corncobs
Dried fruit
Egg cartons (shredded)
Flour products, fruitcake
Gummy bears
Halloween candy
Hay
Icing
Jellybeans (sugar)
Ketchup
Leaves
Muffins
Newspaper (shredded)

Onion skins
Paper, paper towels
Quantity = 40 to 50 percent
Raffia
Stalks & stems, straw
Toilet paper tubes
Used napkins, tissues
Underpants (cotton)
Vacuum (no synthetic
rug fibers though)
Wool
Xerox paper
Yard debris (chopped up)
Zweibach, zero, zone

No-No's
Ashes
Bones
Charcoal
Dairy products
E-coli (fresh cowpies)
Fat
Grease (e.g., bacon)
Herbicide-treated weeds
or grass clippings
Ice cream
Junket
Kefir
Lint (synthetic fibers)
Meat
Needles, pine (acidic and
decompose too slowly)
Oils
Pet poop
Quilts, quackgrass
Rugs (synthetic fibers)
Sawdust (too acidic)
Thistles (spread by root)
Urethane
Velvet and velour
(synthetics)
Weeds with seeds or
roots that spread by
rhizome
X This No-No List
Yogurt
Zippers

The author and a bouquet of kale.

Chapter 4

CONTAINERS

"When I pass a flowering zucchini plant in a garden, my heart skips a beat."

—Gwyneth Paltrow

When my kitchen compost bucket is full, I continue to jam in food scraps on a daily basis, wondering if and when my husband will get the picture and take the bucket out across the backyard to our beautiful new four-tiered compost bin built just last summer by his capable hands.

I have to laugh when I think about how I continue to stuff fruit and vegetable scraps into that bucket. A few of our university/commercial kitchen buckets (given to us by the college where my husband works—any restaurant will gladly give you a used commercial-size sour cream container if you ask) have literally cracked because of my stubbornness!

Sometimes, I glance longingly at beautiful, sleek, kitchen compost buckets in catalogs and on websites, and think how I could integrate such beauty into my kitchen. But then I get sidetracked by working, cleaning, hanging out my laundry (my goal is to never to use the dryer, unless I have towels to dry), socializing, gardening, weeding, etc., and I just don't get around to ordering one. And really, the old plastic bucket is just fine.

Regardless of your design tastes, you just need to have something convenient in which to collect veggie scraps and fruit waste. My bucket is ugly and utilitarian, but it does the job.

POLITICALLY CORRECT COMPOST

I'm master composter, and I wonder if this means my own compost should be "Politically Correct" compost with no half-decayed woolen socks in it. Since 1993, my compost has been inspired by Vera Work, a social worker and Holocaust survivor, who offered a weekend workshop on post-traumatic stress disorder while I was studying to be a mental health counselor at Antioch University New England. Vera brought in a jar of compost that included a large rusty nail, a bit of rag, and a chicken bone. The message to the traumatized client was clear: everything eventually composts.

For years, I threw old ripped woolen or cotton shirts or sweaters into my compost—clothes that had no future even in a big yellow Planet Aid box. I thought decrepit clothes could aid the soil of my garden instead.

But then, digging into a three-year-old compost bin, I'd shovel out a more or less whole green sweater matted with fibrous roots. Maybe it wasn't wool after all? A braided rug decayed into one or two foot lengths. I'd pull out the partial braids and snake them into the neighboring bin where I'd run into the blue strands a year or two later. The leather remains of a moccasin from Alaska lined with rabbit fur—I had worn holes in the sole at the heel and the ball of the foot. A shred of a filmy cotton blouse my mother gave me for Christmas in 1977 still floats around my vegetable garden.

Now, when I pull what remains of a leather glove or a hot pad out of the compost, I put it in the trash bag that's headed for the dumpster. I wonder what archeologists a thousand years from now will make of a grimy, dirt laden, and ripped black cotton t-shirt?

I've stopped throwing my ratty old clothes in the compost. Instead, I toss a hole-y wool sock into the trash. I'll toe the line and keep a politically correct compost. No clothes. Just naked compost. —Cheryl Wilfong

Compost Bin Plans

The most beautiful and practical compost bin ever!

Last summer, I finally said goodbye to my handy old Darth Vader compost bin. It had lasted over a decade, and I was getting tired of shoveling the humus out of the bottom and straining my back.

I convinced my husband to take a few hours off to help me build a new one. If you're handy with tools, allow yourself about three hours to build this, after you have all the materials and tools together. (If you're new to building things from scratch, it may take you half a day.) All the materials are available from Home Depot or any good lumberyard. Cost for all new materials from Home Depot: about fifty dollars, not including the finish.

The picture below of the inside corner of the finished compost bin actually gives you everything you need to know to build this bin. Every corner is identical. It really is a gem of a compost bin!

Materials Needed for the Best Home-made Compost Bin Ever

The author's finished pieces, ready for assembly!

- 8 - 5/8" x 6" x 6' cedar fence boards (caution: don't buy the pine ones that are stained and treated to look like cedar, and make sure your boards are flat and square with no twist or warp)

- 1 - 1-lb box of #10 x 1 ½" hex/washer self-drilling screws

- 1 - 10' cedar 2x4"

- 1 - quart finish (your choice)

Tools Needed

- Power drill with nut-driver bit (to fit a #10 screw)

- Hand or power saw (I used a small saber saw—use a tablesaw or radial arm if you have it!)

- Measuring tape

- Pencil

- "Poly Square" plastic carpenter's square (not necessary, but sure is handy!)

Step-by-Step Instructions

1. Cut the fencing cedar into sixteen 28"-long pieces.
2. Cut sixteen 7 ½"-long pieces from the 2x4. (Cut them about a pencil line's width less than 7 ½", or you'll be a quarter of an inch short of lumber when you get to the last one.)
3. Make a little "jig" (a pattern) that will make it easy to evenly space the legs down 1" from the top of the board while attaching them. Take a scrap of the leftover cedar fence board, and cut it to 6" x 2 ⅛". Cut a 1" piece (as close to 1" and as square as you can cut it) off the end of a scrap of 2x4, and screw it onto one end of the 6 x 2 ⅛ piece you just cut. The picture below shows the jig on the right.

This jig doesn't get attached to anything—it is just a spacer block to allow you to easily screw the legs onto the boards exactly 1" down from the top, quickly and consistently, without having to measure each one each time.

4. You are now going to make sixteen identical leg/board units (pictured on the left in the photo above). Use the little jig to position the leg 1" down from the top of the board, and screw the leg on through the board. Use three screws, positioned as shown in the picture.

5. Now you're going to assemble the leg/ board units into the four independent tiers that will make up your homemade compost bin. It helps if you have a second pair of hands to help you hold things square when you screw the corners together.

Use two (not three) screws on these sides, positioned so that they do not run

into the three screws already in place (see outside corner detail photo below).

After two sides are screwed together, the corner should look like this (it's upside down with the leg sticking up):

The author stands proudly next to her finished composter.

I didn't have a second pair of hands, so I laid them out on a flat patio and pressed them up against a roof post so I could put my strength behind the drill to drive the screws.

At any rate, when you have four of these screwed together at the corners, you have the first tier of the homemade compost bin made. Make three more exactly like it, and you have become the proud owner of your very own *Best Homemade Compost Bin Ever!*

See more at: http://www.vegetable-gardening-with-lorraine.com/compost-bin-plans.html

Compost in a Bucket, a Space-Saving Approach

(This composting method is ideal for apartment dwellers or those with little backyard space to a full operation.)

Materials
- 5-gallon bucket with lid
- Trowel or spade
- Tarp
- 1 gallon of compost, soil, or sawdust
- Compostable materials (grass clippings, paper, food scraps from participants)
- Non-compostable materials (e.g. plastic cups)
- Water
- Worksheet
- "Greens" and "browns" (see Background for "Building a Compost Pile," pages 13-14)

Background Information

Soil is one of the Earth's most precious natural resources. It is composed of rocks, minerals, living organisms, and organic matter. Organic matter in soil comes from the decomposition of plants and animals. Minerals in soil are needed for plant growth. The nutrient cycle, which converts dead plants or animal tissue into a form that can be absorbed by new plants and animals, is essential to all life on Earth.

Tiny microscopic animals in soil eat and transform the dead tissues of plants and animals into nutrients easily absorbed by plants. These bacteria are the most numerous creatures in the world.

One handful of soil can contain five billion creatures, as many as all the people in the world. It happens anywhere there is sufficient organic matter, moisture, and air to nurture the microscopic bacteria, fungi, and other organisms that decompose organic matter.

It is important to maintain the buckets by opening and turning the material with

a trowel every few days to keep the compost aerated. It is also a good idea to add more browns than greens to your bucket. It will not heat up as fast, but it will avoid potentially bad odors.

THE CARE AND TENDING OF COMPOST BINS

The experts say you should layer your compost with equal amounts of green and brown; you should turn your compost; and you should chop your compost into bits and pieces.

But my compost pile is not the focus of my life. I want to be good to the environment and good to my garden, but I also want to be good to my back. I am never going to be turning over my compost pile with a pitchfork. I don't have a spare teenager around the house to send outdoors with a shovel to work off some steam. I am not going to be putting my compost on a cutting board and slicing and dicing (or hacking and thwacking) like Julia Child. I just don't have that kind of time in my life. And I don't expect you to either.

Instead, I do my best at layering the green and the brown as I go along. In the spring and the summer, there's a lot of green. In the fall, there's a lot of brown. Sigh. My "layers" are thicker (way thicker) than what the university extension service recommends.

I do make an extra effort to add a lot of green. Rhubarb leaves are excellent for this purpose and so are carrot tops. Dividing the plants in your perennial garden, as hard as it is, and tossing the extras into the compost is another excellent source of green.

Manure also counts as "green," even though it's brown. If I have the inclination or the time or the truck, I add a big slug of manure to the bins at any time of the year. But definitely in November, I pick up a load of manure at the local farm and use it to "top off" three bins of compost that have already reached the brim with fall clean-up. Then they can sit and "cook" all winter.

Since you and I are not turning, watering, or chopping up our compost, the actual decomposing of the compost will take longer. We are simmering our compost, not roasting it. Therefore, it won't cook as fast as the gourmet compost. But both varieties will "taste" the same to the garden.

Let that heap simmer in its own juices for a year or two. Don't rush it. Just simmer down, my friend. In order to "tenderize" our compost, we are tending it by being tender to it and to ourselves. —Cheryl Wilfong

INTERVIEW WITH ALYSSA HOLMES, MEDICINAL GARDENER

I've been a gardener all my life, and then really got into it through my college experience. I got my bachelor's degree in Sustainable Agriculture at Sterling College in the Northeast Kingdom of Vermont. It was during this time that I knew I would continue to garden for the rest of my life! I have been growing food, herbs, and raising some animals ever since, and composting is a huge part of all of this.

I live on a 10 acre homestead, and I consider it an organism. It all works together, and ideally, at times, a closed loop can be created. This loop can only be created by the building of soil through the maintenance and use of compost.

Now—though I studied compost in ag-tech classes in college, and have visited many places that are doing it masterfully and scientifically—I choose to take a pretty laid back approach. Here on Harvest Hill where I live, we have laying hens, so they get to eat a lot of our food scraps, but many go onto the compost pile as well. At the end of the season, before winter sets in, we clean out the chicken coop (where they spend their nights) and this partially composted chicken manure goes onto garden beds along with leaves and other crushed garden matter. By spring—through all the frosting and heaving and thawing—it is fully composted. It's magical, really.

I strive for a little more organization in the compost realm—like this book suggests—because when we're too lax about it and not aware of materials and the carbon to nitrogen ratio, funky things start to happen! Rats! Sliminess! And squmpkins (squmpkins are those cross-pollinated squash/pumpkin/zucchini seeds that sprouted). Right now in fact, we have squmpkins taking over the pile and ravaging it for all its nutrients. This is a sure sign that the pile isn't hot enough, and in our case, has too many nitrogen-rich materials and not enough carbon (the dry stuff).

We usually apply finished good compost onto the garden beds after one year of successful transformation. It's just soil at that point, but the best of the best! So the trick here is to know how old each of the piles in the rotation is, and also to make sure we chop and turn frequently.

I've had issues with smelly compost inside and flies—we're still trying to figure this out. I suppose I can just buy a fancy counter-top compost container, rather than using a bucket with a lid that does not quite fit!

Urban composters in Tribeca, New York City. *Photo by Vitaliy Piltser.*

Chapter 5

URBAN COMPOSTING

"I'm a chef, I'm a cook, I was created by this industry, and I like to think I'm giving back. But I'm not giving back because I can make a scallop soufflé, I'm giving back because I can make compost."

—Arthur Potts Dawson

Just because you don't have a sprawling backyard and room to spare doesn't mean you can't get in on the composting—and help our Earth at the same time! There are composting systems suitable even for cramped city kitchens, whether you have a full balcony garden, a windowsill herb collection, or you just want to reduce your impact on local landfills.

For those who don't have room for full composting systems in their backyards, smaller systems that don't take as long to produce composted earth can be suitable alternatives. There are many options—some use microorganisms to speed decomposition and others use electricity to generate heat and cut down on waiting time. Traditional compost containers designed specifically to fit in tight places are another alternative.

Urban gardeners are sometimes concerned about the smell of collecting compost indoors or the prevalence of pests.

Many cities, such as Seattle and Portland, Oregon, to name two, provide curbside composting programs and will collect kitchen scraps from participants as they would collect recycling. Other cities mandate that their residents compost; San Francisco collects six hundred tons of compost every day since making composting mandatory.

For those who want to keep their waste out of landfills but don't have a garden (or houseplants) in need of fertilizing, these programs can be very helpful. In cities without municipal programs, compost can sometimes be donated to local community gardens, farmers markets, nurseries, or even given as gifts to friends with gardens!

Bokashi

According to Stuart Franklin, the co-owner of The Green Buffalo and Nature's Lawn & Garden in upstate New York, composting is part of his family's daily life. He uses the *Bokashi* method, which is a tub in which you put your fruit and vegetable scraps, which is basically like "pickling your garbage," he says.

Bokashi (Japanese for fermented organic matter) is a good hands-off option that can be tucked away under your sink or in some corner of your kitchen. The key to Bokashi compost is the microbial powder that is sprinkled on top of compost material. After the microbes get to work fermenting your scraps, you're left with soft, bio-active material which can be added to a garden, fed to worms or a traditional compost pile, or used to create a "soil factory." When the material is mixed with dirt, it quickly breaks down, leaving rich soil behind with very little time or effort. Since the fermenting process happens in a sealed container, there shouldn't be a pest or smell concern and you can compost things in it that would not traditionally be a good idea (i.e. meat, small bones, etc.). Weeds and diseased plants are other traditional no-nos that can be added to the Bokashi system! Although most compost piles don't heat up enough to kill diseases or seeds, the acidic environment created by the fermentation process will keep those concerns at bay. Fermentation is perfect for people who don't have enough space or time for turning and sorting through waste, as this method is not concerned with nitrogen/carbon ratios.

Stuart adds that the tub ferments and kills off diseases without the addition of the usual compost rotting smell, and there is no nutrient loss. When your bucket is done, there is a light mold on it, but it isn't broken down. You can bury the contents right in the ground, or dump it outside in a compost pile. You can also put the contents in a tub of soil and let it break down that way. In the long winters of upstate New York near Buffalo, Stuart keeps and stores a few tubs in his basement until spring. In summer, he keeps the bucket near the compost pile outside. You can collect the juice, and use as a fertilizer—it is very bioactive and has lots of nutrients, but he noted that it must be diluted, because the liquid smells bad and is very potent. The way he composts is he saves up the scraps in the kitchen for a few days, and then they are put in the bucket. He usually keeps two going at once—once one bucket is full he lets it ferment for two to three weeks before burying, while filling up the next bucket.

The Bokashi method is terrific for apartment dwellers or winter use. You can make your own "soil factory" by mixing it with good soil in a storage tub, where it will break down completely within a matter of weeks.

GARDEN SURPRISES

It's a good thing I like surprises.

Last spring I took buckets of compost to my community garden plot. I planted only winter squash and onions there, since I figured they wouldn't need much care, and I only visit once a week. By July, I had a forest of tomatillos growing among the squash. That didn't surprise me. My compost has jillions of tomatillo seeds.

Meanwhile, most of the "weeds" were growing in my onions beds were flowers. I dug out eight dozen Nicotiana (flowering tobacco) and one dozen Verbascum (a sweet perennial mullein that is only two feet tall). I didn't have the heart to weed out Cleome (spider flower), Nigella (love-in-a-mist), Chinese forget-me-not (Cynoglossum), or the opium poppy (Papaver somniflorum) that blooms in late June. Trying to have

The community garden at the Putney Food Coop, Putney, Vermont.

both flowers and onions was counter-productive, so I had to separate them like rambunctious children.

In September, I harvest three winter squash, bushels of tomatillos, and growing right beside the garden gate, ground cherries! Also called Cape gooseberries, these little yellow-orange globes combine the sweetness and size of berries with a hint of tangy tomato-pineapple. Hiding in a paper husk, these little treasures love the heat of summer. I offer these surprises-from-the-compost to my community garden mates and watch them smile at the surprising taste and gift of little berries so late in the growing season.

In October, it's time to pull out the tomatillo bushes, the squash vines, and all the dead flowers, and put them in the compost bin. Perhaps you have a pretty good guess as to what I'm going to find growing in my vegetable garden next summer.

You just never know what surprises your compost has in store for you. —Cheryl Wilfong

Compost in the City

"Composting is when you throw all of your garbage outside in a lidless box, right?" said *every* New Yorker with whom I've ever worked. Aside from the saints of the community garden world, I'm not sure who out here in NYC is turning eggshells and leaf litter into gardener's gold.

I know that urban composting exists and that it is a worthy and gratifying endeavor. But my stories of urban composting have been nothing but hilarious failures. I've stood on a massive twelve-foot mountain of "compost" created by a prestigious landscaping firm trying to be greener only to eventually shovel it all into a dumpster. "This is too hard, too gross, and we're probably doing it wrong" was the general consensus. We were definitely doing it wrong.

I live in Brooklyn, Manhattan's bohemian sister. You can compost here even if you don't have a garden. You can compost just because you want to go the extra mile in your recycling habits. We have farmers markets where you can bring your compost, have it picked up and taken back upstate by farmers who fertilize their crops then sell vegetables back to you at the farmers market. You can then pat yourself on the back for contributing to the magical carbon cycle. Like many professional gardeners here, I do not have my own garden and am waaay too self-absorbed to compost charitably for somebody else's benefit. As far as my clients

Photo of Courtney Wilder by Ian McNaughton.

are concerned, it is hard for the city's rich and glamorous to wrap their minds around the concept that trash contributes to beauty; therefore a compost bin is a rare, almost mythical, object in an Upper East Side garden. There is a stigma, a stereotype, about one who composts. The perceived divide is something like those who buy bulgur and drink out of old mason jars and those who don't. One of my favorite clients, a true and perfect lady of Park Avenue, was being teased over tea by her friends about her style being a little too "Brooklyn." She immediately retorted "Yes, but I'll never compost."

I have, at times, used a well-known fertilizer called Nature's Wisdom "Liquid Compost," that I believe yielded favorable results. It works like a concentrate that you mix in your watering can and you use like any water-soluble fertilizer. Ideal for the container garden, which is my specialty, this particular product is derived from mostly chicken manure and unsurprisingly smells terrible. I certainly enjoyed utilizing Nature's Wisdom without having to turn and stir a pile of half-decaying banana peels and worm colonies, but I also felt I wasn't getting the same, gratifying results that a real composting gardener achieves after mastering the craft.

**—Courtney Wilder,
Professional Gardener who lives in
Brooklyn and works in Manhattan**

GREENMARKET IN NYC

In New York City, shoppers at select Greenmarkets can drop off fruit and vegetable scraps for composting. The program is extremely successful, and really making a difference. Their slogan is, "Make landscape, not landfill!" Here are some highlights, courtesy of GrowNYC:

Why compost?

Food comprises about seventeen percent of New York City's waste stream. When this material is sent to a landfill it contributes to NYC's disposal costs and can create greenhouse gas emissions. When composted, food scraps and other organic waste become a useful product that adds nutrients and improves the quality of soil for street trees, gardens, and more.

Photo courtesy GrowNYC

Photo by Erik Martig

What happens to food scraps dropped off at Greenmarket?

Your household food scraps will be transported to one of several NYC compost sites to be transformed into a fertile soil amendment for use on local urban farming and gardening projects.

Can businesses drop off materials to compost?

No. Commercial food scraps are not accepted at these sites. Businesses should contact a hauler who can handle commercially-generated organic waste.

What can I bring to the compost collection sites?

Accepted materials include fruit and vegetable scraps, non-greasy food scraps (rice, pasta, bread, cereal, etc.), coffee grounds and filters, tea bags, egg and nut shells, pits, cut or dried flowers, houseplants, and potting soil. [Please NO meat, chicken, fish, greasy food scraps, fat, oil, dairy, animal waste, litter or bedding, coal or charcoal, coconuts, diseased and/or insect-infested houseplants/soil, or biodegradable/compostable plastics.]

Photo by Jessica Klajman

How should I store my food scraps?

Food scraps can be collected in large yogurt containers or other covered plastic containers, plastic bags, milk cartons, or in commercially-available compost pails. To reduce odors at home and at the Greenmarket, store items in the freezer or refrigerator. A layer of shredded newspaper at the bottom of your storage container also helps.

Photo by Christina Salvi

The food scrap collection tent is stationed next to a drop-off for clothing and textiles at the Grand Army Plaza Greenmarket in Brooklyn.

GOING GREEN AT THE MARKET

Note: This article, by GROW NYC's Laura MacDonald, first appeared in the Summer 2014 issue of *New York Organic News*, the quarterly publication of the Northeast Organic Farming Association of New York (NOFA-NY)

  Promoting social and environmental issues at farmers markets reflects the growing trend of "green living."

  Stroll through your local farmers market, and you'll be surrounded with the season's bounty of fresh fruits and vegetables, local dairy, and meats. It's easy to become lost in a sea of bright summer berries or mesmerized by huge heads of lettuce still specked with moist soil, a reminder of just how recently that lettuce was growing in a farmer's field. These days, however, more and more farmers markets are becoming not only showcases where local farmers, fishers, and bakers sell goods but also neighborhood centers of sustainability. GrowNYC's Greenmarkets are proud pioneers of this movement. GrowNYC has introduced sustainability centers under bright orange tents at many of our fifty-four New York City Greenmarkets. The centers are run by Greenmarket's sister program, GrowNYC's Office of Recycling Outreach and Education. At select Greenmarkets, New Yorkers can drop off food scraps for composting; unload old clothing, cell phones, and rechargeable batteries for recycling; and learn about other recycling resources, all while supporting the environmental benefits of purchasing food from regional farms.

Photo by Vitaliy Piltser

COMPOSTING: A NATURAL FIT

Farm-fresh produce at a farmers market often comes packaged as nature intended, with skins, husks, leafy tops, and seeds intact. Food-scrap composting at greenmarkets has proved a natural fit and huge success with city dwellers who are happy to tote pumpkin guts and coffee grounds alike to their local market to feed a garden and starve a landfill. Begun as a pilot program with funding from the New York City Council, GrowNYC's food waste collection program has demonstrated the potential to divert a significant amount of food scraps from disposal through composting. In partnership with

Photo by Meghan Kanady

the NYC Department of Sanitation (DSNY), the GrowNYC & DSNY Food Scrap Compost Program launched in April 2012, and today thirty-five Greenmarket locations collect food scraps forty-one times weekly.

  Our urban composters save their fruit and vegetable scraps, non-greasy food scraps (rice, pasta, bread, and cereal), coffee grounds and filters, tea bags, egg and nut shells, pits, cut or dried flowers, houseplants, and potting soil. They stockpile the material in reusable containers and paper or plastic bags, store them in their freezers to prevent odors, and bring them to market on buses, trains, or bikes, or even on foot. The food scrap compost crew ensures that the bins of collected materials are then sent to one of several local composting sites to be turned into a rich fertile soil amendment for use on urban farming and gardening projects. Each week the compost crews break records with the amount of food scraps collected, even in the middle of winter. To date the program has diverted more than two and a half million pounds of food waste from landfills and introduced thousands of New Yorkers to the practice of composting.

RECYCLING IS IN STYLE

Many greenmarkets also offer a place to drop off textiles such as clothing, shoes, and linens. Items collected at a market tent are sorted for reuse or divided into different grades for recycling into rags, insulation, and fiber for car-door panels. As an added incentive for saving those textiles from the trash can, all donations are tax deductible and donors can ask for and receive a receipt. Since the program began in 2007, 2.6 million pounds of textiles have been collected for reuse or recycling at twenty-six greenmarkets, with more locations planned in the coming year.

Photo by Erik Martig

TECHNO TRASH

In November 2009, GrowNYC expanded its recycling efforts at select Greenmarket locations by adding collection boxes for rechargeable batteries and cell phones. GrowNYC established this recycling program in cooperation with the Rechargeable Battery Recycling Cooperation (RBRC), a nonprofit public service organization that operates the Call2Recycle program. With technology evolving at a rapid pace, people are replacing their cell phones every few years, thus creating a huge amount of technology waste. Many cities, including New York City, have implemented laws prohibiting rechargeable batteries and certain electronics from being discarded in landfills. Greenmarkets have proven to be convenient locations for unloading these items for recycling.

LEARNING BY EXAMPLE

Photo by Vitaliy Piltser

Photo by Vitaliy Piltser

Beyond just places for people to drop off their food scraps, old t-shirts, and cell phones, sustainability centers serve as information hubs where shoppers can get answers to recycling questions and find resources such as collections for electronics and harmful household products, as well as GrowNYC's hugely popular Stop 'N' Swap® community reuse event.

Greenmarkets also host one-off programs offering shoppers the opportunity to learn about other ways to live more sustainably. At-market tutorials on indoor composting with worm bins have been a pull for those wanting nutrient-rich soil for their own plants and gardens. At "That's not trash, that's dinner" demonstrations, shoppers

Volunteers process food scraps collected at Brooklyn Greenmarkets at the Added Value Red Hook Farm.

learn how to cook delicious dishes that make use of frequently discarded parts of fruits and vegetables. Some markets also host popular Halloween costume swaps and feature community-based programming, such as eyeglass collections, paper-shredding events, and pop-up repair shops.

Greenmarket's success incorporating programs like food scrap composting and recycling at markets has shown that there is an appetite for the farmers market shopper to connect with more than just their local farmers each week. Farmers markets are no longer just places you can find fresh, healthy, local food; they offer eco-minded individuals a one-stop shop for gaining the knowledge and tools to help reduce their ecological footprint. Helping the environment while loading up on the fruits of Mother Nature's bounty—sounds like the perfect way to spend a Saturday morning.

TIPS FOR ESTABLISHING A SUCCESSFUL SUSTAINABILITY CENTER

- Start by contacting your local municipal waste and recycling centers. They can be a great resource, offering existing programs you can partner with or help in finding facilities that accept particular items for recycling, such as rechargeable batteries.
- Look for community groups, churches, charities, or businesses that might benefit from what you want to collect; they may be willing to provide the infrastructure for the program in exchange for collection materials.
- Establish a realistic schedule and stick to it. Develop a system to quickly communicate any changes to the collection schedule to avoid wasted trips and discouraged recyclers.
- Dedicate someone to oversee logistics, such as monitoring tonnage collected to ensure an ample supply of collection containers and trucks to transport materials.
- An adequate and knowledgeable staff is a must. Train employees and volunteers on what can and cannot be accepted, how to prevent onsite contamination, where materials end up, and who benefits. Encourage them to be vocal and energetic.
- Outreach and advertising is very important. Make your drop-off areas stand out with banners, A-frames, recycling demonstrations, and displays of items accepted. Provide printed postcards and post information online.

Photo by Meghan Kanady

Photo by Meghan Kanady

Photo by Meghan Kanady

Recently, in Brooklyn, New York, composting was made easy by giving each apartment or brownstone dweller a freezer compost bin with which to collect scraps of veggies, and even dry food scraps like pasta and bread, by setting up a weekly municipal collection. The chance to watch the process of the green waste and the brown waste doing the dance of decomposition is missed but nevertheless the urban composters are contributing to the noteworthy goal of cutting out organic waste in the landfill.

According to the Urban Garden Center, "Small batch composters, such as the Urban Compost Tumbler (UCT), fit nicely into an urban setting where people have neither the space nor the time to maintain a traditional backyard compost pile."

It is a good idea to see the process of composting to fully appreciate it. Organizations like GrowNYC offer workshops and tours so urban residents can really see how it all works and what a great benefit it is.

COFFEE GROUNDS, WHO KNEW?

According to the Environmental Protection Agency, many coffee shops, restaurants, and individuals throw away their food scraps, including their used grounds, to the tune of thirty-six million pounds of wasted food that reach landfills each year! If coffee grounds are composted the way one Washington, DC entrepreneur named Eric Steiner does, they help create the ideal soil climate for plant growth, instead of releasing methane as they break down in landfills. In a recent news article about Eric, journalist Heather Brady writes, "Few people are building coffee composting businesses specifically to make a profit from using the nation's widely available supply of grounds."

After more than a decade of producing compost, Steiner has been selling it to suburban gardeners for three years through the grounds-focused company he created, EarthBrew Compost. It's a one-man operation, run with a bright red pickup truck and a tiny patch of land at the back corner of a farm in Brookeville, MD.

Eric Steiner wheels the bin outside to the bed of his truck and begins putting bags of used grounds in it. Photo and story by Heather Brady, WTOP contributor.

Once Steiner mixes the used coffee grounds and horse manure that he collects into his pile, he lets it sit. The one he is making now has been breaking down since May and Steiner feeds it each time he picks up more waste.

When it is done, he will be left with rich, dark compost to sell next year. He keeps two piles at the farm in Maryland and each pile can grow to be more than 20,000 gallons in size. Steiner is developing one pile for future years and selling the other, a finished pile, to customers now.

The forty-six-year-old Baltimore resident intends to scale his business up, taking advantage of the growing popularity of compost and urban gardening. Steiner's secret recipe, coffee grounds and horse manure topped off with vegetable scraps, works particularly well. The grounds provide a large amount of carbon, while the horse manure contains just enough nitrogen to maintain a balance between the two elements.

Photo by Meghan Kanady

Photo by Meghan Kanady

Food scraps from greenmarket collections are composted in windrows on Governor's Island in New York City.

Urban composting is a relatively new trend. In cities that have active composting programs, like San Francisco, composting is thriving and the benefits are not only cost-saving, but they are rewarding to the landscape and the participants.

When I lived in Cambridge, Massachusetts, I put my name on a waiting list for a community garden plot. It was a long waiting list, but eventually I got a very small plot, about 4' x 9'. I was eager to get started.

I drew sketches and planned raised beds for this little plot. Gardening was one of my favorite things to do, and during the spring before my first child was born, I went over there every day. Working in the soil, with my pregnant belly balanced on my knees, was very satisfying.

The year before, when I was in Seattle, I composted and had a year-round garden, mostly in containers. My landlady gave me permission to expand my garden to the curb and I had vegetables growing right along the sidewalk!

If you live in an apartment or a small house in the city, don't be discouraged. You can accumulate food scraps and put them in a bucket in your kitchen. Then, you can add the food scraps to the municipal program like GrowNYC. If you want to try composting at home to enrich the soil for houseplants or a small garden on the patio, you can try using a worm bin, which takes up very little space and is wonderfully efficient.

If you want to get started right away and use compost for your community garden or your urban collection area, you can just store the food scraps in your freezer so they don't smell. If you don't think you cook enough to compost, think again. One individual who composts can really make a difference!

According to Californians Against Waste, compostable organics make up 30 percent of California's overall waste stream, contributing more than twelve million tons annually to the state's landfills. In landfills, this material undergoes anaerobic decomposition and produces significant quantities of methane, up to 80 percent of which is not captured by a landfill gas system. Composting, on the other hand, is a fundamentally aerobic process, and well-managed compost facilities do not produce any methane.

Chapter 6

WHAT DO YOU DO WITH IT?

"Live in each season as it passes; breathe the air, drink the drink, taste the fruit, and resign yourself to the influence of the earth."

—Henry David Thoreau, *Walden*

Whether you diligently turn your compost, or adopt a layering technique, after you have adding the proper ingredients, you should be left with soft, dark, crumbly earth that is ready to be used by plants. Compost can be mixed with existing soil, added on top, or soaked in water to create liquid fertilizer.

Compost is called "soil amendment" when it is mixed with soil to create optimum growing material for your plants. Compost used as a soil amendment should be applied and incorporated into the soil before planting crops, grasses, or plants. For best results, use only finished compost as a soil amendment. This can either be to increase the nutritional content of the dirt or to balance soil that is rich in clay. Compost can be mixed with potting mix to plant seeds or seedlings (the young plants can't handle direct compost) or added to the soil as you dig your garden beds for built-in fertilizer.

How to Use Compost

There are many ways to use compost. Some of the most common uses of compost include:

- Soil Amendment
- Mulch
- Potting Mix
- Compost Tea

Use Compost as a Soil Amendment

Use compost as a soil amendment to increase the organic matter in the soil. For best results, use only finished compost as a soil amendment. Organic matter is critical for plant development and growth (see benefits

The author used compost mixed with potting mix for this Globe Amaranth by her front door.

of compost). Tropical and subtropical soils are notorious for their lack of this material. Whereas temperate soils may have up to 50 percent organic matter, sub-tropical soils typically have 1 percent or less. Compost can help raise organic matter in soils.

Because tropical and subtropical soils never freeze, microbial activity continues year-round. As a result, organic material is used up quickly. Because of biological soil activity and year-round warm weather, gardeners are advised to apply compost annually, or as needed, to increase soil organic matter content.

For best results, use only finished compost as a soil amendment. Compost used as a soil amendment should be applied and incorporated into the soil before planting crops, grasses, plants, etc. Apply one to three inches of compost to the soil surface and work it in to the soil to a depth of about three to four inches.

Plants already in the ground can benefit greatly from mulching, or adding a layer of compost on top of the existing dirt. The compost acts much the same as fallen leaves, keeping the soil protected from extreme temperatures and dehydration. And, as your garden is watered, the compost will provide your plants with nutrients for growth. For houseplants that are already potted, sprinkling a layer of compost on top of the existing soil will keep them looking fresh and green.

Another way to provide your plants with the nutrients they need is by using your compost to brew a pot of compost "tea." The nutrient-rich liquid can then be fed to your plants to provide moisture as well. One reason to make compost tea is to spread the benefits of the compost over a large area.

It is crucial that you allow your compost to finish decomposing entirely before feeding it to your plants. If you add the compost too soon the bacteria it contains will compete with your plants for nitrogen. This can result in stunted, yellow plants and seedlings.

How to Make Compost Tea

Compost tea is a liquid fertilizer that can be used on plants and seedlings to deliver necessary nutrients and suppress plant diseases and fungal activity. Compost tea can be brewed by soaking mature compost in an equal part water and simply stirring, every day, over a period of days or by a slightly more complicated system that uses tubing to aerate the mixture. You can customize your tea depending on what type of plants you plan to use it on. Some gardeners add molasses to increase bacterial production, for grasses, while others add liquid seaweed or fish oil, to encourage fungi, which is particularly beneficial for trees and shrubbery.

The idea behind the concoction is that by allowing compost to brew in the water, sometimes with added seaweed or fish oil, the beneficial microorganisms in it will have the chance to flourish before being applied to the plants. Applying a liquid fertilizer to plants, instead of solid compost, can deliver your plants necessary nutrition as well as hydration. While the scientific community has not officially decided on whether a cup of home-brewed tea will "hit the spot" for your garden, there is much anecdotal evidence that shows—and happy gardeners who claim—that compost tea is well worth a try!

Compost as Tea

Compost tea is a method of using your compost nutrients for indoor plants, potted plants with no room for additional soil, and foliar applications (spraying on plant leaves).

To Make Compost Tea, Follow This Procedure:

- **Step 1** - Fill a woven bag (e.g., burlap) with finished* compost.
- **Step 2** - Place the bag in a barrel or bucket of water.
- **Step 3** - Let sit an hour.
- **Step 4** - Remove the bag.
- **Step 5** - Use the resulting liquid, "compost tea," to water plants.
- **Step 6** - Empty the contents of the bag into the garden and use as compost mulch or soil amendment.

The Benefits of Compost Tea

Compost tea extracts nutrients and microorganisms from the compost and allows you to apply these beneficial components to plants. Therefore, compost tea acts as a weak liquid fertilizer, low in nitrogen but high in micronutrients.

If your plants are container grown, there may be no room to add compost to the pots. Additionally, soil should not be built up against the stems of many plants. Therefore, compost tea is a good option for applying the benefits of compost to container grown plants.

*Using unfinished compost is not recommended due to possible pathogens and compounds that could damage plants. Only finished compost should be used.[1]

_____

1 *Source: University of Florida Composting Center*

COMPOST TEA

After brewing the mixture, you need to strain the tea. Use cheesecloth and strain the tea/compost mixture into another bucket. (You can put the compost solids back into the compost pile or in the garden.) The tea should smell sweet and earthy. If it smells bad, do not use it on your plants, but dump the mixture back into your compost pile.

Apply the compost tea to your flower and vegetable plants immediately. The beneficial microbes will begin to die shortly after the air source is removed.

You can sprinkle the compost tea onto the foliage and the soil around each plant. The tea will provide nutrients and an energy boost to your garden plants. You can apply compost tea every two weeks to your garden.

FOOD PYRAMID

The Healthy Eating Food Pyramid recommends people eat three or more servings of vegetables every day plus two or three servings of fruit. We can serve the same balance to our compost pile: more or less equal servings of green, leafy vegetables balanced with the carbohydrates of sweet fruit plus the high fiber of woody stalks and stems. A plant-based diet is healthiest not only for us, but for our compost pile as well.

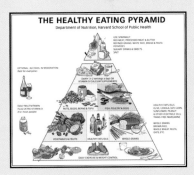

The Healthy Eating Pyramid encourages us to eat a balanced diet for the well-being of our bodies. Our compost pile also works best if it has a balanced diet of green (nitrogen) and brown (carbon and carbohydrates). —Cheryl Wilfong

How to Use Compost as Mulch

Compost is nutritious and attractive when used as mulch. Once your compost has completely decomposed and is dark and crumbly, you can spread it onto your beds as you would mulch (being careful not to touch stems or leaves with the wet compost). The compost will release nutrients more quickly than wood mulch

so will need to be replenished more often (about once a year) but your plants will be better for it! Using compost as mulch will also mean that you don't have to worry about the fungus which wood sometimes harbors. Spread two to four inches depending on your climate. Those in arid climates should use more, while those is cooler climates don't have to use as much mulch. Be sure to give your plants space—four to six inches around trunks—so that they do not become "pot bound." This can happen when plants don't spread their roots because of high nutrient mulch being right near them.

How to Amend Your Soil with Compost

Does my soil need amendment? There are tests one can conduct to identify the exact type of soil you have and whether it needs nutrients, but the easiest way to tell is just by getting your hands dirty! The next time you're in your garden, burrow your fingers into the soil. Is it cool, moist, and crumbly? Can you dig with just your fingers? If the answers are yes, then your soil is probably good. If not, try adding more compost! Compost can help soil with clay or sand bind together to provide better drainage or help retain moisture. Even soil without clay or sand can often use some help from compost for better drainage.

Use compost as a soil amendment to increase the organic matter in the soil. Organic matter is critical for plant development and growth (see benefits of compost, page 11). Compost can help raise organic matter in soils.

Because tropical and subtropical soils never freeze, microbial activity continues year-round. As a result, organic material is used up quickly. Because of biological soil activity and year-round warm weather, I recommend that gardeners in warmer climates apply compost annually, or as needed, to increase soil organic matter content.

END OF GARDENING SEASON

When the growing season is over, but you still have a little let's-go-outdoors-and-garden energy, you can still twiddle your green thumbs by using the last of the thin fall daylight to sprinkle or shovel compost onto your flowerbeds.

November in colder climates is a good time to get a head start on spring. In the spring, the garden becomes a hive of activity. It's good to do as many of those spring chores as possible in late fall, sort of like prepping for a big dinner party by doing some things days (or, in this case, months) ahead.

Go ahead and use up all the compost you have. Compost, unlike a savings account, doesn't accrue interest in the bin. The return on your investment comes from spreading it around on your flower or vegetable gardens. And a good time to do that is when the plants are falling asleep for the winter.

Two seckle pears from the author's fruit trees, and one lone tomato from the harvest in the fall.

Yes, it's chilly outdoors, but you'll warm up quickly by exercising those big muscle groups. Even if your compost isn't warm, you will be.

When I come indoors on a fall afternoon, in my dirty garden clothes, my sweetie hugs me and says, "You smell good. You smell like the outdoors."

Your compost smells and feels like delicious earth. And you are wearing the fragrance of happiness. —Cheryl Wilfong

If you already have a garden that needs a bit of a boost, add some compost, then mix it in a couple of inches deep. This should revive your garden without needing a lot of digging. (If you've already mulched, just move the mulch aside and then replace after mixing.)

With either method, be sure to always mix your compost evenly, as opposed to simply adding it to the plant's hole, which can result in poor drainage as well as roots that never spread.

Unfinished Compost

Using unfinished compost as a soil amendment may stress plants, causing them to yellow or stalling their growth. This is because the decomposition process is continuing near the plant roots and the microorganisms in the compost are competing with the plants for nitrogen. You may want to compensate for this nitrogen imbalance by adding nitrogen fertilizer to soil applications of immature compost.

As an alternative, use compost as a mulch, and you don't have to worry about whether the compost is "finished" or not. This is because any additional decomposition is occurring above the root zone. The plants still benefit from the compost.

Compost as Mulch

The forest floor is a natural composting system in which leaves are mulch on the soil surface, and then gradually decompose, recycling nutrients and conditioning the soil. Likewise, yard debris such as leaves, grass clippings, or shredded branches can be used as mulch in the landscape and allowed to compost on the soil surface. Over time, the mulch will compost in place.

Finished or unfinished compost can be applied as a mulch three to four inches thick on the soil surface. Do not incorporate into the soil. Keep compost mulch two to three inches away from plant stems. Nutrients will filter into soil, without robbing nitrogen from the root zone. The benefits are similar to those of regular mulch: soil moisture retention, insulation from extreme temperatures, and nutrients and organic matter for soil structure. One disadvantage of using compost as mulch is that it will not act as a barrier to weed growth, but, in fact, will promote weed growth if not covered with a standard mulch material. Compost or mulch should be reapplied yearly to replenish the decomposing layer.

Compost as Potting Mix

Compost can be used as an excellent potting soil for your container nursery. Compost offers good water retention qualities and some basic nutrients. However, gardeners should use only fully

COMPOST PARAPHERNALIA YOU DON'T LIKELY NEED

I think I've bought every single piece of compost paraphernalia in the catalog:

- a black plastic composter
- compost aerator (a giant corkscrew)
- compost activator
- compost thermometer
- a sifter
- shredder
- compost bin cover

After all that shopping, I don't use any of these gadgets.

I need shovelfuls of compost, and when I realized that the bottom outlet of the black plastic unit was only big enough for a trowel, I put the composter on the sidewalk with a sign that said "Free." It was gone in fifteen minutes.

About the compost aerator, well, I just never found the time to stand at the compost pile and twist the big corkscrew into it. After seven years of seeing the aerator lollygagging around the compost bins, I finally took it to the Swap Program at the landfill. My trash is now someone else's treasure.

The compost activator is a waste of money. Microorganisms already exist in your kitchen scraps and in your dirt. They will activate your compost just as well as something from a bag or a jar. Just shovel a scoop of dirt on your pile and voila! The vast number of microorganisms that are in the dirt are now in your compost pile and maybe some worms, too. You also can read the label of the compost activator to find out what's so active about the "activator." You can buy the ingredients, such as blood meal and bone meal, at your garden supply store.

I never even tried my compost thermometer because it was pretty obvious that my compost pile was frozen in the winter. The summer temperature was the same inside the pile as out.

The sifter also hangs around the compost pile. I use it a few times a year when I need fine compost to add to potting soil.

Yes, I actually bought a used leaf shredder and used it once. Since I do not relish dealing with mechanical equipment, I sold it on Craig's List two years later and, fortunately, broke even.

A compost bin cover—what was I thinking? I have a roll of black plastic sitting in my basement that I can cut to size and cover my finished compost.

Oh, those compost gadgets are so enticing. They're so beautiful when they're new. Enthusiasm and my credit card carry me away. But now I'm older and wiser, and my compost pile just carries on and does its own thing, never missing all those costly gadgets. —Cheryl Wilfong

decomposed (called "finished") compost as a potting mix.

Container grown plants need a potting soil that retains moisture, but is well drained. Most gardening enthusiasts blend compost with coarse sand, perlite, vermiculite, etc. to make optimal planting media.

If your compost still has large chunks in it, but is otherwise finished, you may want to filter the compost through a 1/2 inch screen to remove un-decomposed material that could rob nitrogen from the plant roots. Smaller chunks in the mix will help maintain a well-drained planting media.

INDISPENSABLE COMPOST EQUIPMENT

A compost bucket sitting beside your sink in the kitchen is an absolute need.

My mother used to have a triangular garbage strainer sitting in the corner of our porcelain kitchen sink. A colander would work just as well.

Nowadays, you can buy a purpose-built little compost bucket with a lid. I bought a ceramic cookie jar twenty years ago. My sweetie broke the lid soon afterward, so my kitchen compost is lid-less. Since we take it out every day, smell is not an issue. The cookie jar "look" hides the garbage contents, so visitors to my home have a hard time finding the compost, even if they're looking for it.

I found a plastic container with a wide mouth (baby wipes, if you must know) that fits perfectly inside this compost/cookie jar. This "insert" is easy to carry back and forth and to wash out.

Five-gallon buckets are the handmaidens of any gardener. For a while, I coasted along on buckets leftover from a construction project. Then I found some buckets at a garage sale. Then I found my next generation of buckets at the farm and garden supply store in the horse department.

Stroll through your garden with clippers in one hand and a bucket in the other. Clip off deadheads, cut down old stems, pick up leaves, and throw them in the bucket. Carrying the bucket to the compost bin constitutes gardener's exercise. Instead of weights, we use buckets for much more interesting repetitions.

I love my garden cart. Mine is forty-eight inches long, twenty-nine inches wide and eighteen inches high. I recommend buying one this size or even a little smaller. Really now, how much heavy stuff do you want to haul?

I prefer the two-wheeled garden cart to a wheelbarrow partly for balance, partly for volume, and partly because you can lift out the front panel and slide any number of heavy items into the cart—garden statues or shrubs, for example. After you've lifted a sheaf of yard and garden waste into the compost, you can easily tip up the cart and let the dirt crumbs slide out. That's what I call easy cleaning.

From summer solstice until fall equinox, I count on my garden cart to haul volumes of gone-by perennials, weeds (pre-seed, hopefully), and rotten vegetables to the compost pile.

Little by little or lot by lot, we just keep adding to our compost pile. —Cheryl Wilfong

Photo by Vitaliy Piltser

VERMONT COMPOST COMPANY

The Vermont Compost Company was founded by organic crop growing professionals in 1992 to meet the need for high quality composts and compost based living soil mixes for certified organic crop production. The mission and principles of the company are formed by concern for the integrity of food and the soil from which it grows.

Karl Hammer of Vermont Compost in one of the green houses.

In 1960, when Karl was eight years old, his parents left their home on Manhattan's West Side with one thousand dollars and drove north until they could buy more than a hundred acres with it. They got as far as Vershire, Vermont, where they purchased 125 acres of pasture and forest at the top of the watershed, for $1,250.

Karl was fascinated with farming from his earliest memories, and in Vershire in the 1960s he found manure-based, horse or mixed horse/tractor powered farms still operating using the traditional methods. From his farmer neighbors, Charles Orr, Bill Perkins, Stanley Kendall, Gile Kendall, Ralph Brown, and others he learned these traditional farming methods, like how to stack loose hay and drive a horse and a tractor. Karl said, "they showed me how to go out in the woods and get the guts of hollow logs in a wheelborrow to feed to hogs. They fed horse and cow manure to hogs. They bedded cows with grass and leaves . . ."

When Karl was in his teens he left public education behind to begin an unusual path. In 1969 he traveled to Spain where he worked with the local farmers and started a bagel baking business. As a teenager he also traveled to New Mexico to farm, and by the time he was 19 he came back to Vermont and began to clear land, starting an organic farm on his family's land in Vershire. He said, "We started farming in 1970. Milking goats, cows, selling vegetables at the farmer's market, Norwich market, and to New England Produce, which later became Squash Valley Produce."

Karl remembers a local Hardwood bobbin mill on a 10 acre river bottom where there was a "library" of different piles of bark, all separated by species and age. With access to this resource he experimented. "When I got there you could buy an eight yard bucket for $2.00. Any species and any age: Ash, yellow birch, maple, oak, all of different ages. When you first clear hardwoods you get incredibly vigorous plants."

With learning partners like the well-known organic grower, Eliot Coleman, who was then at the nearby Mountain School, Karl began to realize that fertilizers and potting soils that were commercially available didn't have any labeling to say what they contained. Karl began experimenting with making his own compost and potting soil.

During this period, Karl also began to read extensively about organic growing. Among his influences were Sir Robert Howard who had developed the "Indore process," named after a town in the Punjab in India, where Sir Howard had farmed in the 1920s. Sir Howard's book *Soil Testament* established one of the central principles of organic farming: "feed the soil, and the soil will feed the plants." From this principle in a nutshell comes the Vermont Compost motto, "Feed the Soil."

Karl has been instrumental in starting a number of other manure processing and composting operations, as well as having begun a large organic farm in Millerton, New York. In 1987, Karl started Moody Hill Farm in Millerton, an extensive greenhouse growing operation that also produced its own compost and potting soils. That operation continues an extensive organic growing operation today, under the name of MacEnroe Organics.

Karl helped to found the Intervale Compost facility in Burlington, Vermont, the manure composting operation at Leemax farms in Hartland, and at Lylehaven Farm in East Montpelier, Vermont. The current Vincent Flats composting facility in East Montpelier operated by Vermont Compost is an integral part of the operations of Fairmont Farms, a large dairy operation. Karl continues to offer consulting services in the development of composting and organic growing operations.

Karl has developed into a compost specialist, a humus connoisseur, who combines a comprehensive understanding of soil and plant science with a practical knowledge of the challenges organic growers face, and an ability to judge a windrow of compost that verges on the sort of magic employed by wine connoisseurs and chefs. Karl sticks his nose directly into a handful of compost and sniffs, like he is sampling fine brandy.

From that potent combination of knowledge, practical experience, and intuitive comprehension, Karl has developed, taught, and largely systematized a process for consistently producing very high quality composts and soil blends.

In 1996 Karl bought the Main Street Farm. Since then Vermont Compost has grown from a small, mostly local operation to a company that now supplies the six largest CSAs in the upper mid-west, supplies Martha Stewart with her potting soils, and is the soil of choice for many of the cutting edge, professional organic growers in Vermont and the northeast. These growers are making money with Vermont Compost products, and so can you.

Farm visit: Green Mountain Girls Farm. Photos from Vermont Compost

Chapter 7

TIMING IS EVERYTHING

"To cherish what remains of the Earth and to foster its renewal is our only legitimate hope of survival."

—Wendell Berry

The first step of composting is just to start. It is easy to get caught up in the science of aeration and bio nutrients, how they break down the material and create the end result—compost as a soil amendment and garden mulch. But at some point, you just have to go for it and begin. A lot of it comes down to common sense.

The compost pile at Miller Orchard near the author's home in Brattleboro, Vermont. Photo by Lynne Jaeger Weinstein.

A mantra for creating a successful home composting system is to tell yourself that you are keeping waste out the landfill and giving back to the earth by improving the soil. A sign of an avid gardener is one who reacts to the question of "Do you compost?" with glee and speaks passionately about it as a newfound avocation.

Recently, I attended an environmental writing conference and got into a lively discussion about composting at the dinner table, it seemed that everyone at the table had a story to tell!

According to the Urban Garden Center, "An important issue with composting in small batches is—when is it really compost? While an oversimplification, since all composts are not the same, if you do everything right, you can produce fresh compost, which is like fresh manure and not aged, in about two to three weeks in many of the fully enclosed compost bins. However, if you want cured compost, which is the process of slow stabilzation after high-temperature decomposition, it will take at least another two to three months. You can empty your compost bin and set the compost aside to cure for two to three months before using. Or, for outdoor applications, just spread/mix it on the ground and let it finish curing in place. For indoor applications (e.g. house plants) you might consider curing it outside for at least thirty days before using it in a living space. Curing time will vary based on temperatures and conditions."

FUNERAL FLOWERS

I like to send flowers to the family when someone dies, even though the obituary says "In lieu of flowers, . . ." Since I like flowers and I like to receive flowers, I just assume other people do, too. I often send the flowers directly to the family's home rather than the funeral home.

To support local businesses, I go to whitepages.com and type in "florist" and the zip code where my friend lives. Then I call and order cut flowers rather than an arrangement. Doesn't everyone already have enough vases at home? I assume my friends do not need another vase.

Photo by
Vitaliy Piltser

Funeral flowers remind us of the impermanence of life. One day, one year, we are in full bloom. A few days or decades later, we start to wilt. And finally death and the compost pile.

Flowers don't have personhood, so we can easily see how decaying compost gives rise to new life. When it comes to people though, our attachment to personhood, to "self" interferes with this simple, straightforward understanding of nature.

Really, how are our physical bodies really any different from flowers? —Cheryl Wilfong

To Air or Not

It isn't a complex procedure and the timing is easy to gauge when you have a chance to look into the bin and mix it up a bit with a shovel. When you add air—oxygen—to the pile it speeds up the decomposition of the organic material by allowing the microorganisms to do their work. If you don't ever turn your compost or create tunnels of air inside of it by mixing in stocks and other larger yard waste, it will still break down and decompose, but anaerobically, or without air. It really is a simple process, but fascinating nevertheless. You get to watch a biology experiment take place in your tiny yard, or worm bin.

STORIES FROM "THE FIELD. . . "
She Loves to Take Out the Compost in the Winter

Diana loves to take out her kitchen compost bucket in the winter even though she has to trek across a hundred feet of snow. While she walks, she is busy looking for the tracks of animals who have been visiting her lidless black plastic composter.

She sees the blue jays fly away. She can hear the crows an hour after sunrise. But she is on the lookout for the calling cards of smaller visitors: mouse tracks, squirrels (both gray and red), foxes (both gray and red), chipmunks (in February and March), turkeys, raccoons, rabbits, and deer. Once in a while, she is surprised by less common visitors.

Diana's neighbor, Lynn Levine, has written an easy and excellent guide: *Mammal Tracks and Scat* (www.heartwoodpress.com), which Diana can refer to if she has a question about who has left their footprint. She herself is so committed to leaving a smaller carbon footprint, that she doesn't mind trekking out to the winter compost. —Cheryl Wilfong

To Turn? Or Not to Turn?

Ben has one compost pile out in the back corner of his yard—just a loose heap unconstrained by bins. Every couple of weeks, he takes ten minutes and turns the pile from right to left, layering leaves and grass clippings as he goes. Two to four weeks later, when he's walking by with a shovel in his hand, he turns the pile from left to right. Basically, he's turning the pile upside down at least once a month.

The key to Ben's ease with turning is that he's not turning his pile in place. He has one compost pile, but two "compost spots," and he's moving his pile from one spot to the other.

Mary Lou gave up on turning her compost piles because she didn't see that turning every three weeks hurried the process of decomposition.

Tatiana calls herself a lazy gardener when it comes to turning compost, but if you saw her tiny organic farm and her dozen compost bins, you would not call her lazy. "I only turn my compost once a year, in the spring," she says. No wonder.

Her definition of "turning" is taking the under-composted top layer off the most mature pile, and throwing it back onto the resting pile or into an empty bin.

"Dig down until you get to the good stuff," she says.

Now it's your turn to decide: To turn? Or not to turn?

Sifting Compost

Mary Lou has a clinker sifter that her father gave her decades ago. Back in the days of coal furnaces, a clinker sifter was used to filter the coal ashes and then throw the bigger, usable bits of coal back in the stove. The round sifter, about a foot in diameter, has a half-inch mesh screen.

She uses the big flat sieve to sift her finished compost. The large mesh holes enable small clods of compost to fall through to the five-gallon bucket sitting underneath. She sifts out stalks and stems and rocks and throws the uncomposted bits back into the "unfinished" compost pile.

I use a flat or plant tray that has solid sides and medium-sized holes in the bottom. I fill the tray with compost and jiggle it over the wheelbarrow.

Mary Lou uses her sifted compost to fill old window boxes. Because compost has a tendency to be dry, she saturates the window boxes with water for a couple of days. Then she seeds them with lettuce, spinach, and arugula in April and again in August. She sets her window boxes in her ratty old greenhouse, where she does have to water the greens in her window boxes every day. She transplants the seedlings into her garden, and harvests fresh greens from April through June and again from August through October.

After sifting through all this advice about your compost, you could buy a fancy sifter from the gardening catalog, but you can also make do with hardware cloth, deer fencing, or a hole-y plant tray as your compost sifter. If you even sift at all.

Lobster Shell Compost

Friends who rent a summer house in Maine come home with a five-gallon bucket full of lobster shells. They've already taken a shovel and crunched the lobster shells into bits to compact them. When they arrive home, they dump the pulverized lobster shells onto the compost pile.

The main component of crustacean exoskeletons is chitin, which can improve overall crop yields by building strong cell walls. Strong lobster shells make strong plant cells. Chitin also induces defense mechanisms in plants, strengthening their immune systems.

Yes, my Maine friends do occasionally find bits of red lobster shell in their garden, but eventually it breaks down.

Seaweed

Ben spends a week at the coast every summer with his family. While he's there, he gathers up five-gallon pails of seaweed from the beach. He gets a lot of weird looks, and people ask him, "Are you going to eat it?"

Well, not exactly. Not as seaweed, anyway.

He hoses the kelp off back at the beach house to de-salt it. By the end of the week he has three or five buckets full of seaweed, which he loads into trash bags and drives back to his mountain home.

Living in the mountains, Ben buys Ice Melt by the five-gallon bucket, so he has a good supply of buckets. He uses the salt in the winter to de-ice his sidewalk, and then, in the summer, he adds de-salted seaweed from the beach into his bucket.

Ben has a smallish compost heap, so he mixes the seaweed into the pile so that he doesn't overwhelm it. Seaweed qualifies as "green," so he layers it with brown leaves.

One great thing about seaweed—it doesn't have any weed seeds!

EVER-GREEN COMPOST IN VERMONT: AN INTERVIEW WITH CO-FOUNDER, SÍLE POST

Síle Post from Ever-Greenhouses, as someone who grows year-round even in the cold harsh climate of northern Vermont, you must require a steady supply of compost. What's your philosophy of composting?

I like to approach my composting as I do my cooking and baking—*Homemade, Local* and always *Organic*. Like the food I prepare from scratch, I make my compost from local ingredients that either I have grown myself, sourced myself, or have identified their origins. My mantra is always *fresh,* always *local and always* organic.

Secondly, I like to be as holistic as possible. As someone who tries to 'live in each season', as Thoreau urged, living according to daily and seasonal cycles, I like to consider how I can recycle on a holistic scale. By heating with wood, baking in a wood-fired oven, and/or by simply enjoying a lot of fires during the long winter months, for example, I recycle my wood ash to my compost, thereby adding a significant level of potassium. (Otherwise, greensand will do!)

I like to use my own homegrown vegetables and food scraps as essential ingredients to my compost. I grow greens year-round, so I am always adding extra greens, legumes and herbs to my compost pile, as well as the spent stems and leaves of my greenhouse produce, hence the term, *ever-green*, as in our new Vermont business, Ever-Greenhouses! (www.ever-greenhouses.com)

The author mixes organic soil with compost for her fall raised beds in the greenhouse where she will grow lettuce and cold weather herbs like cilantro, parsley, and arugula through the winter.

Síle Post, I am so happy I now own one of your first greenhouses and plan to start my seedlings for lettuce in the fall and tomatoes in early February. Tell me about your philosophy of composting since you are a master gardener and composter.

A holistic approach to composting is really about creating a loop that regenerates itself.

All our greens go to waste—through composting. During the summer months, when we are 'growing' our compost, we use the top layer to grow, in turn, squash, which *loves* growing atop compost! When we're ready to harvest the squash, we simply turn in the remains of the plants, adding to its richness.

Síle Post, I want to try this next season!

I also grow medicinal flowers and herbs, as well as perennials. When fall arrives, and the flowers have gone by, I turn them into the compost as well, adding essential nutrients to the compost. Nothing goes un-re-used!

What are some of the advantages to your local, homemade approach?

I like to maximize the health of my soil and subsequently, my fruits, vegetables and herbs. I like to think about composting from a common sense point of view: Can rotting vegetables that contain deleterious substances, such as GMOs and res- idues from chemicals and drugs, be eradicated in a heating process? I studied enough chemistry in college to know if I want (even organically labeled) compost that is chemically free of such residues, I must make it myself!

What's your secret recipe for ever-green compost?

I add to the compost four seasons a year. In addition to my wood ash (for potash), extra cool and cold season greens, such as Asian greens, mustards, spinach and kale, for example, grown in the cool (and cold) greenhouse provide much-needed winter nourishment for my com- post pile. During summer months into fall, all extra and leftover warm soil vegetables, fruits, flowers and herbs are added as they mature.

While all (organic) food scraps find their way to the compost year-round, I enhance the pile by adding an addi- tional level of nutrition—what I call 'earth elements.' For the micro-nutrients and trace elements, I use seaweed that I dry myself, or when unavailable, add dried kelp meal, while other essential earth elements such as boron, I add directly to the pile. Boron, available as borax in North America, has been shown to contain amazing health benefits including hormonal balancing, increased bone density and anti-arthritic qualities.

And as you have pointed out, compost benefits immensely from finely ground eggshells, from organically- and pasture-fed laying chickens!

Finally, I go a-gleaning, as we say up here. Various weeds actually contain powerful medicinal qualities and nutrients. I compost entire stands of wild Burdock, which grows in abundance, as well as various other seasonal weeds and wildflowers.

Let's put it this way: From such composting practices, I've been able to preserve 135 quarts of tomato sauce each fall, just by growing in my family's own ever-greenhouse!

Thank you, Síle, for your insights. I'm looking forward to growing in my new greenhouse this winter!

See information about this new approach to year-round gardening and compost- ing in the Resources section.

Kids with compost bucket having fun at a Highfields (Vermont) school workshop.

Chapter 8

COMPOSTING IS EASY

"The glory of gardening: hands in the dirt, head in the sun, heart with nature. To nurture a garden is to feed not just on the body, but the soul."

—Alfred Austin

While composting is fun and educational for adults, it can be especially so for kids. When we compost, we learn about and are connected to the larger world as well as our local habitats and even the food we eat. Composting can be an entertaining way to introduce basic scientific principles to younger children and can help develop more advanced concepts for older children. It requires problem solving, creativity and—best of all—playing in the dirt!

Composting requires four things: oxygen, appropriate temperature, moisture, and a proper carbon to nitrogen ratio. Learning about each of these parts and how they work together to create rich fertilizer for plants can help children become better connected with their Earth as well as understand the world around them.

If your compost is going into a vegetable garden that provides you with food, your children will not only better understand where their food comes from, but also will be more invested in it. Try involving the kids in the cooking, too!

Kids can do anything—and everything—from sorting their scraps into a collection bucket to helping to turn the pile to spreading it in a garden. Although they will need guidance, and often physical help, from adults, their interest can help motivate you to take care of your pile!

Preschool

For the youngest kids, composting can begin at meal times. Explain which food scraps can be composted and which ones should be put into the garbage. (If your food scrap collection bucket is kid-friendly, your little one can even be responsible for putting their scraps directly into it.) While their arms may be too small to help turn the compost, letting them watch and introducing them to the "creepy crawlies" who live in the compost will help them begin to understand where their food comes from.

Elementary School

Composting is an excellent way to teach students about the life cycle: birth, death, decay, and rebirth. When we teach composting, we are teaching how nature recycles. Students learn that by composting, they care for their communities and the natural environment. By adding compost to plants, students learn that healthy soil makes healthy plants and that all humans and animals depend on healthy plants to live.

As your child gets older, the composting experience can increase from mealtime participation to playing in the garden. When the food scrap bucket is emptied, you can explain where food would go if it wasn't composted and what the benefits of composting are. Even those who cannot fully understand the math and science behind composting can begin to develop an appreciation and responsibility for their earth.

If you have a couple of square feet of soil to spare, your child can experiment with his own composting! Have him collect his food scraps separately and then at the end of the week take them out to your spare land. Insert six wooden stakes into the ground about a foot apart. Your child can dig a hole at the first stake, bury his scraps, and return to do the same thing at the second hole the next week. By the time she has filled all six staked holes, finished the cycle and returned to the first stake his first buried scraps should be decomposed! For children who are interested in the way the world works—and who like playing outside—this can be a perfect introduction to decomposition without having to worry about mixing the materials. If your child is interested, let her plant some simple plants between the stakes and see firsthand the benefits of composting. Let your child experiment with what she buries, how deeply, etc., and perhaps even keep a journal about what she "discovers."

Middle/High School

By middle school many kids are developing a sense of responsibility for their Earth. Composting can be a great way

Maia Hansen, the Outreach and Education Coordinator at Highfields

Tell us a bit about yourself.
My name is Maia Hansen. I am twenty-six and work as the outreach and education coordinator at Highfields Center for Composting. I started school at Whitman College in Washington State and transferred to the University of Vermont, where I graduated with a BA in biology and a minor in geology.

What is your personal experience with composting? How did you get interested in it?
I've been composting all of my life, so the practice of separating food scraps is purely habit. I grew up in a very rural community with a lot of woods and not much else. My idea of fun as a kid was "fishing" in mud puddles, hiding in the pea plants, and making rock houses for snakes and toads. I spent countless hours helping my parents spread compost on the garden, plant seeds, weed, and harvest vegetables. I've always been fascinated by the way a plant grows and what it needs to be successful.

Since working at Highfields, I have learned so much about the organisms that live in a compost pile and the symbiotic relationships that make nutrient uptake by plants possible. Yes, I work with dirt, but it is living, breathing, vibrant dirt that has countless benefits.

Do you know how to compost indoors? Do you have any experience with that, personally?
My only experience composting indoors is in keeping a worm bin. My household worm bin, which is also my travel worm bin for training sessions, was built by a group of students and has been working great! I use a simple plastic Rubbermaid-type bin with holes drilled in the top, sides, and bottom. I feed the worms vegetable peels once every week or two and add plenty of moistened strips of newspaper. Our

Maia Hansen, Close the Loop! Regional Coordinator. Photo by Vchem Pierce

office worm bin has had more issues with fruit flies and my research on this subject shows that fruit flies are attracted to low pH conditions, so keeping acidic foods (like citrus and coffee grinds) out of the bin is key. Worms break down material pretty quickly, but they don't need much to keep them busy, so keeping a compost bucket/bin for the majority of kitchen waste is still necessary.

Any tips for troubleshooting smelly compost, dry compost, and other problems?
If a compost pile is smelly, it is usually too wet or too nitrogenous. Quick tips are to add plenty of carbon-rich materials such as dried leaves, dried garden material, hay, woodchips, or peat moss. Having a stockpile of these materials helps, especially in the winter. Aerating a pile is also crucial in keeping it from going anaerobic (without oxygen) and producing methane. Turning or fluffing a pile with a pitchfork can usually remedy this problem.

I've been living off the grid for the last three years and so I've also been composting urine with peat moss. I find this can be smelly, but letting it sit without any turning gives the nitrogen-fixing bacteria plenty of time to convert the ammonia. I usually let it sit for at least six months before adding it to my compost pile, and then give it at least another six months to decompose further. I worried about burning my plants with too much nitrogen, but my garden seemed pretty happy with the soil!

How and when do you apply the compost to your garden beds? How do you put the garden to bed and/ or wake it up in the spring?

We usually apply compost to the garden in the spring after we've tilled in the winter rye and beds have been made, making sure to incorporate it deep enough into the soil, but also being careful not to spread it in the walkways where weeds will monopolize the nutrients. As we harvest, we replace portions of the garden with a cover crop—typically buckwheat and field peas during the growing season. In the fall, we rototill the cover crop into the soil and replace it with winter rye. Acid lovers like blueberry bushes are mulched with pine needles on top of the compost.

Any funny stories about composting? We like those a lot!

Going into schools to teach kids about composting is perpetually a treat. Students seem most shocked to hear that compost is jam packed with bacteria (one billion bacteria in one teaspoon of compost) and that these tiny creatures are capable of producing such hot temperatures (160 degrees F)! Disgusted looks aside, this information sticks with them.

My all-time favorite story came from a kindergarten class that was learning what happens to our food scraps if they end up in the landfill. I asked what the name of the gas was that goes into our atmosphere from the landfill. I gave them a hint, starts with an M. Hands flew up and we called on a boy who stood up in excitement stuttering . . . "Muh, muh, muh . . . MOIL!" I hated to break to him that he was combining the word soil with methane and we didn't bother to mention that a "Mohel" is, in fact, the man who performs circumcision.

for a person to not only feel connected to the planet that provides for him but also to take care of it. This is a good age to share more of the composting responsibility as well as more of the technical side of composting. Experimenting with ratios can be a fun, hands-on math experience while turning and spreading compost can be meditative and relaxing—you can also get some extra energy and help with the turning process with an easy activity that kids can do with a shovel and supervision. If your child gets excited about composting, ask how she would feel about teaching others how it works. She can start a composting program at school or ask local businesses to leave their coffee grinds out for composters. People who are passionate about an issue can bring about real change, and it's wonderful for young people to experience this firsthand.

College Age

Oberlin College students recently initiated a new composting system in their dormitories and housing. There are now fourteen compost hubs on campus that student volunteers coordinate. At the forefront of this program is the Oberlin College Resource Conservation Team (RCT), a seven-member student group employed by the college to reduce waste production on campus.

The RCT manages this new program with the help of student volunteers called Compost Captains. Since the program is in its first year, only fourteen compost hubs were accepted. The program is modeled from the new sustainable freshman dorm on the Oberlin campus, Kahn Hall, where the entire building has been composting food waste since August 2010. Compost Captains coordinate the location of the bins within the dorm or the student house and teach the students living there about what can go into the compost bins. The education component is important because it familiarizes students with compost systems and requires them to reflect before throwing something in the garbage.

Each week the RCT picks up the compost bins from the fourteen locations and drives the compost to the student garden, Johnson House Garden, which uses the compost throughout the year. The food from the garden is sold to the student dining halls and to the student cooperatives on campus. This closed-loop system will educate Oberlin College and peer institutions about the possibilities for compost and local food.

The RCT hopes to expand the program within the next few years depending on the success of the fourteen compost hubs on campus. Eventually, every dorm may have a compost system so that recyclable waste and food waste are all dealt with properly. Properly disposing of waste, including compost, will reduce Oberlin College's environmental impact and provide a working model for peer institutions to follow.

From Food to Flowers

New York's Ithaca College began composting food scraps from its dining halls in January 1993 using an aerated static pile system installed in a forty-by-eighty-foot steel building on campus. Food-scrap composting was instituted as a solid waste management strategy that would reduce the cost of land filling. An added benefit is the production of a small amount of high quality humus, an excellent soil amendment.

In October 2000, operations funded with a matching grant from the New York State Department of Economic Development began in a new compost facility designed specifically to meet the needs of the college.

All food scraps, including plate scrapings, are collected in "food only" containers located at food preparation and dishwashing areas.

Full containers are taken to the trash collection areas at dining hall loading docks. These containers are emptied into a forklift mounted dumpster that is used for daily collection.

Currently, the college is collecting and composting about twenty cubic yards (20,000 lbs) of food scrap per week, or approximately 20 percent of the total waste stream.

After extensive experimentation with compost to soil ratios in seed germination, transplants, and field tests, a mixture of one-third compost to two-thirds topsoil is used in all ornamental planting beds on campus. Compost is also applied as a top dressing to lawns.

Irene Canaris, *Westminster West School Garden, Westminster West, Vermont*

Award-winning Vermont educator, Irene Canaris, with one of her students at Vermont's Westminster West Elementary School.

Tell us a bit about yourself. How did you get interested in working with kids and growing a school garden?

When I was eight years old, I organized the kids in my neighborhood to plant a flower garden in our backyard, and when I was twelve, my grandmother helped me to plant my first small vegetable garden beside her house. Ever since then, I've had a vegetable garden at home. I became a teacher in Vermont in the 1980s, when I was in my early twenties, and one of my student's parents was a young organic farmer. When he saw what kids were bringing in for morning snacks, he suggested planting a small vegetable garden outside our classroom door as a way of showing students where real food comes from. After twenty years of successfully growing our large two-classroom garden and healthy snack program, a new principal helped us create an "all school garden" for 170 students, grades K–6. A parent wrote a grant for an all school healthy snack program and now all students get a daily free nutritious snack. I retired from classroom teaching a few years ago and I'm now "rehired" as the Westminster Schools Garden Coordinator.

Elizabeth Ungerleider

Tell us what you can and can't throw on your compost pile.

No meat products; they take too long to decompose and attract carnivorous animals (dogs). Any vegetable matter can go into our compost. I would imagine that if we begin composting in earnest next year, I would contact local mills to obtain clean sawdust. This is a helpful addition to compost. I would also get the support and guidance of farmers who've been composting for decades.

When we "put the garden to bed" each fall, students join together to clear large organic matter from our garden (like sunflower stalks and cabbage roots). This helps ready us for tilling so that we can plant winter rye to add nutrients to the garden in the fall. It's a great way for kids to see how teamwork gets things done more efficiently and pleasantly. It's also a good opportunity for students to move around outdoors. Physical activity promotes focus; good learning results from this complement to endless classroom sitting. They also make great connections between what's

on the compost pile and what those same plants looked like last spring—the cycle of life, death, and regeneration.

Do you have any experience with how to compost indoors?

When we first started our large classroom garden, we weren't allowed to build a compost area outdoors, so we created a worm farm in our classroom. It was so successful that we donated worms to other teachers who wanted to start classroom composters. The kids could measure how much of their cantaloupe rinds, for instance, were eaten over the weekend. Fruit flies were a big drawback, however. We would vacuum them out of the air every week or so.

Elizabeth Ungerleider

What challenges have you run into with composting and gardening at the school?

Our all school garden is far enough away from the school now so that school board members probably wouldn't raise the same issues against outdoor composting that they raised years ago. Their concerns back then were that compost would attract vermin and it would smell. (Actually, composting materials have a pleasant smell. It's all in how you approach things.)

A problem with having the garden so far from the school, though, is that kids can't get all the way out to the garden daily during the snowy winter months in Vermont.

We have a new custodian who is on board to help explore composting options for us this spring. I'm hopeful that we can get rolling with our composting program.

When and how do you apply the compost to your garden beds?

Compost takes many forms. Winter rye, once it grows to a certain height, fixes nitrogen into the soil. It can be planted after harvest in the fall. It is then cut down and becomes an important part of our garden mulch.

In the spring, we have dairy farmers and organic farmers/parents in our community who volunteer to spread manure and to till our garden in May for our June Planting Day. Children love to watch these big machines do their work. (Our garden is 75x150 feet . . . a lot of growing space.)

The kids help us spread composted mulch over the garlic beds we plant in November. The best compost is horse manure or rabbit manure because there are no hayseeds in it. Hayseeds tend to create more weeding work in the summer months. We mulch with straw. It keeps moisture in and keeps weeds from growing between rows.

Elizabeth Ungerleider

Photos by Elizabeth Ungerleider

Students at Westminster West School in Vermont are active composters and educator, Irene Canaris, has established an interactive program that stimulates health, intellectual curiosity, science, and fun.

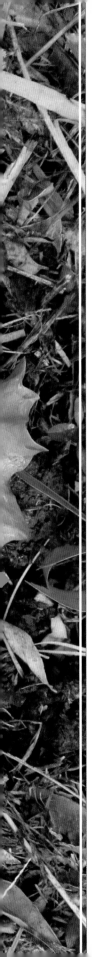

Chapter 9

WHAT GOES IN YOUR PILE, GETTING STARTED, AND TROUBLESHOOTING

"A garden requires patient labor and attention. Plants do not grow merely to satisfy ambitions or to fulfill good intentions. They thrive because someone expended effort on them."

—Liberty Hyde Bailey

Now that you've learned the basics of composting, you are ready to get started. This chapter is devoted to the practical steps for creating a stress-free environment for your brand new organic composting system. Remember, whether it is chicken wire and a few posts and a staple gun, or wood pallets stacked in a square, your compost pile is part of the whole process.

According to Susan Antler, the executive director of the Compost Council of Canada, "An important first step to getting started is to place your composter in a sunny area with good drainage. Make sure that the location is convenient and accessible year round."

GETTING STARTED . . .

- Turn the soil under which the composter will sit.
- After placing the composter, cover the floor of it with a layer of small branches. This will allow for air movement and drainage.
- Alternate wet (e.g. kitchen scraps) and dry (e.g. yard material) waste.
- If available, add some "finished" compost, garden soil, or a compost starter (available at most garden centers) to the pile. This helps speed up the composting process.

CONSTIPATED COMPOST

You know what too much roughage (and not enough water) in your diet leads to: constipation. Your compost pile can also get constipated with too many stalks, stems, and dead plants. In composter-ese, this impacted condition is called "too much brown."

Dousing your pile with water might help, but it can also lead to compost diarrhea—a very unpleasant gooey mess with attendant icky smells.

The remedy for dry and scratchy compost is to add more vegetable matter—more green—into the diet of your compost pile. Kitchen scraps are an easy solution, unless you are concerned about varmints. The suburban gardener can add grass clippings (if the lawn has not been treated with chemicals). Add big green leaves such as rhubarb leaves, squash leaves, carrot tops, or bolted lettuce. If you're not getting around to eating your kale and collards, add those. They're as good for the digestive health of your compost as they are for you. Manure will also solve the blockage.

In any case, it will probably take a few months for your compost pile to relax its cramped belly. Be patient with your sickly (or stick-ly) compost. It just needs to get some rest. Continue feeding your cold compost healthy doses of greens while you wait for the cold to run its course. Time heals all. —Cheryl Wilfong

Clues on Composting

- The composting process works best when the organic pieces are small. Weeds and trimmings should be shredded.

- Don't add thick layers of any one kind of waste. Grass should not be more than 2 ½ inches deep, leaves up to 6 inches deep (cut or chop or dry and crumble them). If you can, let grass dry first or mix it with dry, coarse material such as leaves to prevent compacting.

- The composter contents should be moist like a wrung-out sponge. If the contents are too dry, it will take overly long to compost; and if too wet, the contents may begin to smell.

- Turn or mix the compost every couple of weeks or each time you add new material. This keeps the compost well aerated.

- Composting can be done in the winter, so go ahead and add materials to your composter all winter long. The breakdown process slows down

SHOULD YOU COMPOST ASHES?

Those of us with wood-burning stoves would love to put those wood ashes in the compost. It seems like such a natural place to dispose of them but don't do it.

Here's why: Ashes are alkaline. They're good for the acidic soils of the Northeast and places that receive acid rain, but they're too powerful for compost. Wood ashes soaked in rainwater for three days creates lye, a caustic potash. We don't want the ashes in our compost to convert to lye and kill the microbes.

It's generally advised to add ashes to the garden in the fall. The problem with this scenario is that we don't have ashes in the fall—we have ashes in the winter and spring. So just sprinkle those ashes directly on your lawn or flowerbeds or on the snow covering them. Ashes are excellent for melting ice, but remove your shoes at the door if you don't want ash tracks throughout the house.

Areas with alkaline soils have absolutely no need for alkaline wood ashes. One possible exception is to kill viral weeds with extreme pH so that nothing will grow on the site where the wood ashes are applied.

We want our plants to grow, but we don't want to overpower them with too much of a good thing, or they may not rise from the ashes. —Cheryl Wilfong

or stops when the pile is frozen, but it will start up again in the spring. Thorough turning in the spring will reactivate the pile. Empty the composter in the fall to make plenty of room.

Troubleshooting

Composting is not difficult but sometimes the process requires a little extra attention. Here are some easy solutions to correct certain situations that might occur.

- If the pile does not decrease in size or generate heat, composting may need a boost. If the pile is dry, add water, mixing it in thoroughly. If the pile is wet and muddy, spread it in the sun and add dry material. Remember to save "old" compost to mix with incoming material.

- If the center of the pile is damp and warm, but the rest is cold, the pile may be too small. Try to keep your composter as full as possible. Mix new with old, dry with wet, breaking up mats and clumps.

- If the pile is damp and sweet smelling but not heating up, it may need nitrogen. Add grass clippings, table scraps, or a sprinkling of organic fertilizer from the garden center.

- If the compost pile develops a foul odor, it may not be getting enough air. Loosen up the pile, break up clumps, unblock vents and perhaps add some wood chips to help the pile "breathe." Turning the pile always helps aeration.

- Keep your compost in a container with a cover to prevent animals from getting into the composting materials.

A wire mesh around the base can help to prevent pests from digging under the pile. Dig in or cover food waste immediately.

THE LIVING DEAD

Although we typically think of our compost pile as composed of dead matter, this is not quite true. A dead tree, for instance, is home to fifty-two species of creatures. And our compost heap is also home to many living creatures, some so small we cannot see them.

Into the compost pile go dead plants and dead leaves, along with rotting fruits and vegetables that have overstayed their welcome in our refrigerator.

What we usually call "dead" is precious life for someone or something else.

Little mites, sowbugs, centipedes, and various larvae come to feast and thereby hasten the process of decomposing. Nematodes, mitochondria, and other invisible bacteria and microbes are also at work, converting death into life. *(Continued on next page)*

When you open your black plastic unit in the spring, stand aside for a minute and let life fly out. Then carry your living compost to your garden, and let life begin to feed the new growth of seedlings and plants.

It's a miracle, isn't it? Life springs from all those dead and rotting plants. It's enough to give us hope.

—Cheryl Wilfong

IS IT FINISHED YET?

The composting process can take from two months to two years, depending on the materials used and the effort involved.

Compost is ready to be used when it is dark in color, crumbly, and has an "earthy" smell. You can sift the compost to eliminate material that has not yet finished composting. Return this back to the pile to complete its transformation into humus.

PUT COMPOST TO GOOD USE

Composting can benefit your soil and plants in many ways. It increases the soil's organic matter content and its moisture-holding capacity. Compost improves soil porosity and helps to control soil erosion. It also enhances plant and flower growth and helps plants develop a sound root structure.

Use it on your lawn, in your garden, around trees, or combine it with potting soil for your plants. *From the Composting Council of Canada.*

THAWING THE COMPOST PILE

It's early spring and my compost pile is an iceberg.

Yes, I know the heap is supposed to be hot, but mine is cold. Really cold. Frozen solid. I managed to scrape two inches off the top before I hit the tundra.

This is just one more good reason to spread compost on the garden in November. Otherwise, when spring rolls around, and you're ready to use it, the compost pile is permafrost.

So now it's time to practice patience. I know the snow bank on the north side of the house sometimes doesn't totally melt until early May. But it does melt. And my compost will thaw out too. My impatience heats me up but does nothing to thaw the compost. So chill out, my friend. The warmth of spring is coming.

My iceberg compost reminds me of how I sometimes prepare dinner. At 5 p.m., I pull a container of food or maybe a frozen chicken breast out of the freezer. How am I going to work some magic on it so dinner will be ready by six? Sometimes I microwave it, but sometimes I put it in a covered saucepan and slowly scrape the thawed part off, layer by layer, as if that will hurry it up. I'm not going to microwave the compost, nor am I going to take an ice ax to it. I just have to wait for the sun to add the heat. —Cheryl Wilfong

COMPOSTING WITH CHICKENS

Chicken manure can be wonderfully beneficial for your plants with more nitrogen, phosphorous, and potassium than either horse or cow manure. It does, however, need to be processed differently from just food scraps and garden waste. Chicken manure—

if used raw—can damage roots, kill plants, and spread pathogens, so it is important to let it fully decompose before spreading. Some people like to have a separate compost system for use with chicken manure, as compost takes much longer to mature when manure is being used. It will take some experimenting to figure out the appropriate carbon to nitrogen ratio, which will depend on the type of bedding you use for your chickens. Due to the high level of nitrogen in chicken manure, you may try mixing it with an equal part brown material or even two parts brown. Since there is a risk of spreading pathogens through chicken manure, it is important that your compost pile heat to a temperature of 130 to 150 degrees and maintain that temperature for three days. (If you're not sure about how hot the core of your compost is getting, you can purchase a compost temperature gauge to help.) To do this, collect about a cubic yard of material in your first composting location, add water so that it is about as damp as a wrung out sponge, and let sit until it has reached the appropriate temperature. After reaching the peak temperature it will begin to cool and need to be turned so that the material on the outside edges can be heated. This should be done three times, after which your pile should be loosely covered and left for two-and-a-half to three months. At that point you should have dark, crumbly, sweet-smelling fertilizer ready to be added to your garden.

The author's compost system.

My compost pile is four feet square and four feet high. It is just my husband and I at home now, so I dump the kitchen scraps for the two of us about once a week. I dig the finished stuff out of the other bin that is further along once or twice a year and that decreases the volume by half when I harvest.

I definitely do not have enough to cover all the plants and gardens around my house, so I recommend applying the composted humus on a rotating basis: you can topdress one area each year and record it in a garden journal. It is a good idea to keep some compost stored to mix with potting soil, to use for potting or transplanting during houseplants and kitchen herbs during the year.

The author composting her tea leaves which she buys in bulk at the local food co-op to save money and packaging.

One of the author's raised beds at her home in Vermont.

The author mixes her aged compost with organic garden soil for her winter greenhouse made by Vermont company Ever-Greenhouses.

The author at home dumping her kitchen compost into her backyard compost bin.

Chapter 10

HOW THE SCIENCE WORKS

"A garden is a grand teacher. It teaches patience and careful watchfulness; it teaches industry and thrift; above all it teaches entire trust."

—Gertrude Jekyll

Keeping Your Microorganisms Happy

Your compost pile relies on a community of microorganisms all living together. When these microorganisms thrive, your compost will thrive as well. There are several factors that we can control to create the most efficient compost possible. One factor is what we add to begin with. As discussed in previous chapters, the two main categories for compost ingredients are nitrogen-rich and carbon-rich components, green and brown. In order to maintain an optimal compost pile (and avoid smelly anaerobic bacteria) there needs to be a balance between the two.

Although the perfect ratio depends on the type of soil to which your compost will be added, thirty parts carbon and one part nitrogen is a good initial ratio. Keeping the nitrogen levels high enough will ensure that your pile heats up enough for efficient decomposition. However, compost piles with too much nitrogen can become too hot, killing the microorganisms living in the piles. If the balance is maintained though, your microorganisms—and therefore your compost—will be able to use these nutrients to thrive.

Since we want to maintain the bacteria, worms, and other organisms which make decomposition possible, we want to not only feed them properly but to be sure not to poison them. This means adding organic materials that are not contaminated by pesticides or fungicides. Even if your microorganisms survive to decompose the material, plants fertilized with compost containing pesticides, herbicides, or fungicides may suffer.

HARVEST: BOUNTY OR COMPOST?

In the harvest season, I try to cook two or three vegetables from the garden for dinner every evening—broccoli or zucchini, chard or kale, and a salad entirely of tomatoes. I leave the leftovers in the fridge for my sweetie. When I return from a long weekend away, they're still there.

"You're supposed to have eaten these," I say, with one eye on the overflowing harvest basket I just brought in from the vegetable garden.

"Oh, I did," he says. "Except for that yellow squash. You deal with that."

This is when the bounty of the garden takes a dive into exasperation. Too much of a good thing leads to some form of stress or other. There's nothing to do but throw the week-old leftovers into the compost. Then I spend an hour after dinner slicing tomatoes for the food drier or blanching broccoli for the freezer.

For years, after reading *The Magic of Findhorn,* I worried that the tomato devas might have their feelings hurt by wasting the food they guarded into fruition. But lately, I've come to see that waste is waste—whether it goes through my digestive system or straight into the compost pile.

And the great thing about waste—human, animal, or compost—is that you can use it to grow more vegetables. Humanure, moo doo, zoo doo, or leftovers—it's not being wasted. It's all just compost. —Cheryl Wilfong

RED RUSSIAN KALE

Russian red kale easily survives our New England winters, so in early April, I harvest enough for dinner. Braised with onions and garlic from last summer's garden, our supper costs nothing. Dinner leftovers from two years ago went into the pile to become compost last spring and spread on the vegetable garden to grow the kale and onions that we eat for dinner tonight. Any leftovers or onion skins go into the compost bucket and . . .

Kale—an exemplar of the circle of life that flows through us. —Cheryl Wilfong

Plant-Available Nutrients and Micronutrients

- As compost breaks down in the soil, it provides the fertilizer nutrients of nitrogen, phosphorus, and potassium in forms that are readily available to plants.
- Unlike most inorganic fertilizers, compost functions as a slow-release store of nutrients, so that the nutrients are available as the plants require them instead of in one intense flush.
- Compost also provides a wide range of important micronutrients not found in commercial fertilizers.

Benefits of Organic Matter in Soil

- Added to sandy soils, the organic matter in compost increases the soil's water-holding ability so that both rain and irrigation water are held in the root zone for plant use. This can significantly lower the irrigation requirements in the orchard industry and other applications where water use is restricted or prohibitively expensive.
- Compost lightens heavy (high clay) soils, allowing better infiltration of both air and water into the root zone. This improves plant health and helps to prevent sealing of the soil surface caused by water pooling.
- Organic matter functions like a sponge, enabling soil to retain nutrients and moisture in the root zone. Inorganic fertilizer nutrients as well as those released by the compost itself are kept from leaching down into ground water.
- Soil structure is improved, allowing effective drainage, extensive root growth, and soil aggregate stabilization, so that soil is less subject to erosion by either water or wind.

- Earthworm activity is encouraged, further enhancing soil fertility.

Biological Activity

- Compost is biologically active, supplying a range of microorganisms that enhance the health of both soil and crops.
- Compost appears to suppress some types of plant disease—the exact mechanism is not yet fully understood.

The author's raised bed garden with healthy soil and healthy organic plants.

NO WEEDS, PLEASE

Oh, it is so tempting to toss the weeds into the compost pile. But don't do it! You're just recycling weeds. This means you need an easy alternative. Where are you going to put your weeds?

In the spring, I do throw weeds into my compost with this caveat: they aren't blooming, and they have not set seed yet. Some grasses don't set seed until late summer, so I can toss their greenery into the compost until then.

But once a weed is flowering (and some of them have tricky green flowers) or definitely when a weed has gone to seed, you really shouldn't compost them in your final bin destined for the garden. Here are some possibilities:

Throw weeds into the woods. I live in the country, so I can throw my weeds into the woods. *Good luck growing in the shade*, I think as I toss them into the trees.

Create a dry-and-die pile. Set out a square of black plastic and put your weeds onto it. On a sunny day, they'll bake to death in just a few hours. Perhaps even cover them loosely with the black plastic so they'll double bake in the sun. A day or two later, you can add your sun-dried weeds to your trash, where they'll take up a lot less space than when they were green. I live in an area where burning is permitted, so I throw my dried weeds onto a brush pile. If you have a fire pit, pitch them in there.

The author's other compost bin, the one she calls "Darth Vader."

Another version of the dry-and-die pile is to use a bucket or a trug that you won't need for the foreseeable future. I have one invasive weed that I call "Enemy." Enemy can gallop through a flowerbed in no time. And here is its secret: it grows from the tiniest rootlet left in the ground. I definitely do not want to spread Enemy around, so I carefully put it and all the roots I can find into a bucket. If I only have one bucketful, I cremate it in the wood stove. But if I have a trug-ful, I let them molder until it's time for my next campfire.

After all, we don't want s'more weeds. —Cheryl Wilfong

Compost as Mulch

When used as a mulch, compost can:

- Conserve soil moisture, reducing the need for irrigation in dry areas
- Minimize weed growth
- Insulate soil to slow temperature changes; dark color may also help soils to warm more quickly in spring and retain heat longer in the fall.

Vermicomposting

An earthworm in the author's garden.

The long, squishy earthworms that children toy with on playgrounds and fishermen use for bait can also be used to make nutrient-rich compost without much effort. In nature, worms naturally feed on decaying organic material but when they live in your compost pile these fertilizer-making machines can be harnessed for the good of your garden.

Worms help keep balance in the soil by providing plants with necessary nutrients and microbes in forms that plants can access. Their connection with soil fertility has long been recognized: Aristotle referred to worms as "the intestines of the earth," the removal of earthworms from Egypt under Cleopatra's rule was punishable by death, and after years of studying them Darwin said, "It may be doubted that there are many other animals which have played so important a part in the history of the world as have these lowly organized creatures."

But what is it exactly that they do? When worms swallow organic material it passes into their gizzards where it is processed to release enzymes that convert the material into energy the worm can use. The excreted waste, or vermicast, is especially high in levels of available nitrogen, phosphorus, magnesium, carbon, calcium and potassium. On top of its exceptional range of nutrients, worms also live in symbiotic relationships with lots of microbes that populate the vermicasts.

Although the idea of raising living worms in your compost pile may sound daunting, it is very easy—it doesn't even require turning, as the worms will do that for you. Worms can be kept inside or outside (depending on your area's climate) and they can be fed most things you'd put into your compost pile. Due to the rate at which worms eat, vermicomposting is much faster than traditional composts and the worms keep it at the optimal temperature. Vermicomposts can be smaller than traditional composts and are virtually odorless so they are perfect for the urban gardener as well.

Setting Up a Worm Bin

More than seven thousand species of worms inhabit the world, and they are important to ecosystems.

Worm composting is an excellent way to introduce living decomposers in the classroom. By keeping an active worm bin inside, students can observe the natural cycles of decomposition and gain new appreciation of earthworms as the "guts" of the soil.

Worms are incredible decomposers. The worms we use for composting in boxes are surface feeders called *eisena foetida*. They are also called manure worms, red wigglers, or redworms. Today, there are engineers in India who are learning how to clean sewage water using worm systems. There are lots of fun facts to know about redworms. They have five pairs of hearts, no eyes, and no teeth. They breathe through their skin, and need dark, moist surroundings. Eight adult redworms can produce 1,500 offspring within six months, if conditions are favorable. Each worm is both male and female and can eat over half of its weight in food every day.

SETTING UP A WORM BIN

Materials Needed (Described below)

- Worm bin
- Bedding materials
- Handful of soil
- One pound of worms
- Water
- Collection container

Worm composting is a fun, low-maintenance way of recycling your organic kitchen scraps. Worms eat your vegetative food scraps, turning them into a high quality fertilizer known as worm castings. You provide the living environment for the worms—the bin, bedding, and food—and the worms do the rest. Worm composting can be done inside or outside (depending on climate), requires no turning, is odorless if done correctly, and can be done in small spaces. Worm composting is most appropriate for food scraps. The compostable matter we throw away—such as apple cores, melon rings, and soggy bread—are things that worms like to eat. Redworms eat food scraps and break them down into rich, dark brown, earthy-smelling material called worm castings. Castings, which are nitrogen-rich fertilizer, can be returned to the earth and are good for lawns, gardens, and houseplants.

Procedure
Buy, scrounge, or build a worm bin:

- A worm bin can be made of wood, plastic, or other materials.
- The size of your worm bin (for home or classroom) should be at least 1-1/2 square feet, and about 16 inches deep.
- Good ventilation is essential for aerobic decomposition and a healthy environment for worms.

Prepare Worm Bedding:

- Tear newspaper into 1/2-inch to 1-inch wide strips (tear lengthwise, with the grain).
- Dunk newspaper strips in water and add to bin.

- Add a handful of soil and fluff.
- Toss everything like a big salad.

Add worms and food:

- Purchase or obtain about 1 pound of red worms (about 500 to 1,000 worms)
- Gently place you worms in the moist newspaper bedding near the bottom of the bin.
- Put a handful or so of food waste near the worms and cover well with the moist newspaper bedding.
- Add more dry shredded newspaper to fill the bin, and then a layer of burlap or cloth.

Using worms to compost our food scraps makes sense for a lot of reasons:

- We will reduce the amount of garbage we create.
- Compost improves the soil and makes it hold water better.
- Using compost reduces the need for chemical fertilizers, which helps prevent the creation of more pollution.
- Composting with worms is fun!

Let your worm bin rest by not adding additional food for one to two weeks. This allows the worms a chance to get used to their new environment and for the food to begin to decompose.

For ongoing maintenance, feed every three to seven days, always burying the food under paper. Do not overfeed. Bad smells or large amounts of uneaten food indicate overfeeding. Add more paper as needed to cover food. Harvest castings after three to six months.

The Worm Bin Environment

The worm bin environment includes worms, bedding, food, worm box animals, food, moisture, and more. Through exploration, participants can learn what worms need to live and how to go about setting up a worm bin. Worms, like humans, need air, water, and food to live, and a worm box should be cool and moist. Worms are amazing animals that breathe through their skins. If their skin dries out, they will die. Worms can eat more than half their weight in food every day. They have no teeth but grind the food in their gizzards. Did you know that they don't have eyes? Worms sense light without seeing it.

A worm box is an ecosystem all in itself. There are many other animals that live in the bin besides the red wigglers. You may see mites, beetles, ants, or sowbugs, to name just a few. All of these animals are important and play a vital role in your worm box.

Harvesting a Worm Bin

Harvesting a worm bin allows you to see the magic of the life cycle and it is a fun family project. By remembering the kinds of foods or other materials that were placed in the bin, we can marvel at the compost (or castings) worms have made. Worm castings are very high in available nitrogen, so they are a high-quality organic fertilizer for plants. There are several methods for harvesting and everyone seems to have a favorite.

For this type of home composting, it is important to have access to a worm

The process show at "Down To Earth Worm Farm" of Greensboro Bend, Vermont, is an indoor vermi-composting facility, where they tend large drawers full of red wiggler composting worms. The worms are feed basic compostables, (i.e., kitchen scraps, coffee grounds, garden waste, manure, leaves, etc.). In turn, they render worm castings (worm poop) which is the best natural plant food & soil revitalizer.

bin, which has been fed for at least three months. Here are the three basic techniques used for home harvesting:

- Bucket method (requires a tarp, bucket, and water)
- Sunlight method (requires a tarp, bucket, and a sunny day or bright light)
- Hand-picking (requires a tarp and bucket)

Bucket Method:

Place all contents of the worm bin in a bucket. Gently pour cool water in the bucket. The worms will be okay for a minute or two. Pour the contents of the bucket through the colander. Retrieve the worms and uneaten food and bedding from the colander and return them to the bin. The brown liquid is compost tea that can be used to water plants.

Sunlight Method:

Mound compost in small piles on the tarp and let them sit in the sun or under a bright light for a few minutes. The worms will move to the center of the pile to avoid the light. The outer part of each pile, now without worms, can be removed and put in the five-gallon bucket. As the castings are removed, the newly exposed worms

will head to the middle out of the light and the process can be repeated until you are left with a ball of worms. This ball of worms can be returned to the worm bin.

Hand-Picking:

You can also sort through one big pile of compost on the tarp, picking out any worms you come across, and return them to the bin. Continue until the pile seems to be relatively worm-free.

Using:

The castings will need to sit for two or three days before they are ready, then they can be applied directly to plants. The compost tea may be put into empty beverage bottles and used right away.

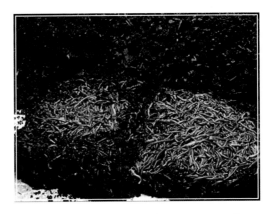

Red Wiggler worms with casings from Down to Earth Worm Farm in Vermont, indoor vermicomposting facility.

THE RON FINLEY PROJECT

Join Ron as he embarks on his next project: igniting a (horti)cultural revolution! Ron envisions a world where gardening is gangsta, where cool kids know their nutrition, and where communities embrace the act of growing, knowing, and sharing the best of the earth's fresh-grown food.

Ron is realizing his vision for community gardening and rejuvenation. Let's grow this seed of urban guerilla gardening into a school of nourishment and change. Help spread his dream of edible gardens, one city at a time. It's time for Americans to learn to transform food deserts to food forests, to regenerate their lands into creative business models! Let's make Ron's philosophy mushroom across the country, and the world.

In part of this effort, Ron is planning to build an urban garden in South Central LA that will serve as an example of a well-balanced, fruit-and-veggie oasis called "HQ." Inspired by the idea of turning unused space such as parkways and vacant lots into fruitful endeavors, this garden and gathering place will be a community hub where people learn about nutrition and join together to plant, work, and unwind. HQ will create a myriad of jobs for local residents and the plot of land will be a self-sufficient ecosystem of gardening, education, cooking, business learning, and management. The community will get their hands dirty together, shovel together, work together, and be healthy together.

MEET RON FINLEY

Ron Finley is a man who will not sit still and watch a problem take root. Having grown up in the South Los Angeles food desert, Ron is familiar with the area's lack of fresh produce. He knew what it's like to drive 45 minutes just to get a fresh tomato. In 2010, he set out to fix the problem. Right outside his front door! Ron planted vegetables in the curbside dirt strip next to his home. And quietly, carefully, tenderly started a revolution.

"I wanted a carrot without toxic ingredients I didn't know how to spell, " says Ron.

His was an exceptionally creative, cost-effective, and simple solution; however, it was also an act of spirited rebellion that led to a run-in with the authorities. The City of Los Angeles owns the "parkways," the neglected dirt areas next to roads where Ron was planting. He was cited for gardening without a permit. This slap on the wrist did little to dissuade his green thumb and Ron fought back. Hard. He started a petition with fellow green activists, demanding the right to garden and grow food in his neighborhood—and the city backed off. This caught the eyes of creative leaders and media voices that lauded his courageous act of ebullient defiance. Ron has continued to share his story and vision with the world, giving a TED talk and planning many exciting ways to continue his involvement in mitigating Los Angeles food deserts.

His dreams have been reshaped into a thriving garden of pumpkins, peppers, sunflowers, kale, and corn. But more than being a guerilla gardener, Ron is a community leader. Determined to change South Los Angeles from food desert to food forest, he wants his actions to be educational, inspiring, and nutritious. He wants kids to grow up with the option of healthy food, instead of fried, fattening staples. He wants to sweep up and transform his street, his hood, the city of LA, and communities everywhere.

http://ronfinley.com

Donations to help Ron pay the staff and continue changing lives can be made here:

QUOTES FROM RON:

"Gardening is the most therapeutic and defiant act you can do, especially in the inner city. Plus, you get strawberries."

"If kids grow kale, kids eat kale. If they grow tomatoes, they eat tomatoes."

"We gotta flip the script on what a gangsta is—if you ain't a gardener, you ain't gangsta."

Chapter 11

USING WHAT YOU MAKE—STARTING A GARDEN OR DONATING TO A COMMUNITY GARDEN

"Nature does nothing uselessly."

—Aristotle, *Politics*

It is hard to imagine ever being able to actually use the stuff you make! After two years of dumping veggie scraps and fruit rinds, eggshells, coffee grounds, tea bag entrails, and other kitchen debris (never dairy, or meat!), I was ready to use what I had made. I was too busy to pay much attention to what was going on inside the pile (now that I have worked on this book I know how exciting those bugs are!), and I just couldn't bring myself to shoveling out the compost and setting up the garden and the flower beds. Building our own house had long been a dream of ours, and when we finally moved in, it was as if there wasn't time or energy to devote to things like painting the trim, or starting a vegetable garden.

I have always loved freshly-cut flowers, so that was one of my first projects: I started a small, sloping flower garden filled with roses and annuals (dahlia, nasturtiums, gladiolas); and then a lower garden filled with annuals, like poppies, daisies, and peonies.

a counter upon which to set up my garden six-packs. The organic soil is store-bought and easy to use for the process of growing seedlings—you want the plants to have a good start, with plenty of sun and water.

I made sure I worked a little bit each day—it helped that my children were getting older and liked to play outside, or read books. And occasionally they would binge out by watching their TV hour (we had strict rules on television watching, but often let them watch longer, though in the summer we disconnected the TV entirely, much to our children's dismay. But I am glad we did!), and I could find a little time to work in the garden.

Many times, I found myself transplanting seedlings in the dark, or in the moonlight, not wanting to use even a flashing light for fear of attracting bugs. It was actually a good time to transplant and water the seedlings, it turns out, to avoid the heat of the day and give them a less stressful start!

It was one of those late afternoons that had offered a respite from the work of a household with three kids under the age of twelve, and I had some time at the beginning of the summer to mix in the new compost with the soil. I didn't buy new soil, as I already had wonderfully rich topsoil I had already

Since my budget for my gardening is small, I did what I could to save money, and found the process to be rewarding in return. I started my seeds indoors in the late winter, early spring. I studied how to start morning glories (a little nick in the seed a twenty-four-hour soak in water would speed up the process), and other indoor seedlings. I have a wonderful south-facing kitchen with a row of windows and

purchased from the local organic gardening center. (I was looking for sales constantly, and even found a place you could drive to a load up the back of your car, or truck, with soil and save a great deal of money—all that was needed was a tarp so your car didn't get dirty, and a shovel).

I remember I worked quickly, and when I mixed in the compost from the black composter bin, I had the sudden feeling of accomplishment, the pride of making something useful and healthy and beneficial.

The rest, as they say, is work, but it is work that yields tangible results.

JOHNNY-JUMP-UPS AS A COVER CROP

The purpose of a cover crop is to increase fertility of the soil, to decrease weeds and pests, and to create biodiversity. Cover crops are called green manure because farmers plow these nitrogen-rich crops into the ground where they improve the soil.

Most cover crops are in the legume family (alfalfa, vetch, clover) or in the grasses family (rye, oats, wheat, or buckwheat), but they also include mustard and arugula of the Brassica family.

Every spring, my vegetable garden and the nearby strip beds are covered in Johnny-jump-ups (Jjus). They're cute, and to me, they're a weed. But now, I've decided I'm using Johnny-jump-ups as my cover crop. Here's why:

- Jjus don't prevent weeds exactly, but each plant covers half a square foot, and nothing grows in the shade of a Jju.
- They bloom profusely in April and May and are a joy to behold.
- In late June, they become leggy, so I pull them out wholesale and fill one compost bin completely full of Jjus. Although they don't fix nitrogen, they add a lot of "green" manure to my compost bins.

Too many Johnny-jump-ups is a win-win situation. You'll have beautiful flowering beds in April and May and an overflowing green compost bin in June to really get that compost working. — Cheryl Wilfong

Planting in Compost

The structure of soil is improved when you add compost, which increases the soil's ability to hold water, helps soil to achieve a good airflow, and adds nutrients for plants. Compost will reduce the risk of plants getting diseases and will give life and vitality to your soil. Healthy soil means healthy plants. Healthy plants mean healthy animals and people. It is possible to do this activity with worm compost. If you choose to do so, keep in mind that worm compost acts as a highly efficient organic fertilizer and you only need to add one part worm compost to two parts soil.

Materials Needed

- Compost
- Empty six-pack planter
- Drip trays for planters
- Potting soil (buy organic soil)
- Seeds, such as bean or sunflower (for beginners, as they are easier to manage, and since they sprout easily)

1. Fill the six-pack containers with one part compost, one part soil.
2. Place three seeds in each of the sections.
3. Water the seeds as directed on seed packet.
4. Set aside in a warm, sunny area.

DEFENDING YOUR COMPOST

The number-one reason people don't compost is fear of varmints. Predator pets—a dog or a cat—that spend time outdoors are your first line of defense against the four-legged critters you don't want raiding your compost. The pet patrol can be very effective at keeping bandits, masked or otherwise, at bay. Cats will crouch nearby for hours, staking out the compost pile for little furry tidbits.

Your pets may never actually take the varmints into custody. Just the smell of carnivore poop and pee can be enough to deter visits from bothersome herbivores who find a compost pile to be a handy grocery store. But you do not want your pets to cross the line and get into the compost themselves. You may have to arrest your dog's tendency to joyfully leap into the bin for a snack. You especially do not want pet poop in your compost.

If your pets abide by the rules you set, they will defend your compost pile against raiders of every stripe. —Cheryl Wilfong

Start a Garden

Even before you launch into the planning, take the time to first ask yourself a few questions that will help determine if a new garden site or group is what's actually needed.

- Is there another community or school garden in your area that is already serving the people you're hoping to reach? If so, is there a way you could support or further their goals?
- Is there a garden group in your area that is open to expanding its reach? If so, could you work with an existing group to create a new garden site?
- Is a community or school garden something that will meet the needs and desires of your community? Is there another project that would better suit your goals?

Stages of Garden Development

Once you've taken the time to think over the suitability of your project, you're ready to start planning! Remember: every garden and every community is unique. With that in mind, there are steps to building a new garden community that many new garden groups have found helpful to see them through the process. Rather than using the following information as a checklist, I hope that these tips can give you guidance where needed. I wish you the best as you begin to build your garden!

- Get your group together.
- Define your goals.
- Develop your garden management plan.
- Pick a site.
- Design your garden site (phased development).
- Develop your garden budget and fundraising plan.
- Build your garden site.
- Grow your team.

Establishing a Garden Project

1. Get your group together.
   - Seek out dedicated, motivated individuals to be a part of your garden planning committee.
   - Engage a diverse group of people that represent stakeholders in your soon-to-be garden.
   - Establish clear lines of communication and regular meetings for the group.
   - Define roles and responsibilities for your garden.
   - Good leadership and management skills will help to build your garden leadership team.

2. Define your goals.
   - Meet as a group to discuss and determine the purpose or mission for your garden.
   - Develop goals that will bring you closer to the overall mission.
   - Identify concrete tasks and a timeline for achieving them. This planning checklist can get you started on your task list and will help keep you on track.

3. Develop your garden management plan.
   - Discuss management roles, gardener outreach, registration, fee structure, etc.
   - Creating community garden guidelines is a great way to get everyone on the same page from day one.
   - When thinking through roles and responsibilities, it may be helpful to think through the year based on monthly tasks.

4. Pick a site.
   Look for a site that meets your garden's purpose and goals. When choosing the potential garden site, keep in mind several considerations, including:

   - **Light**: At least six hours of direct sun daily.
   - **Drainage**: Little to no standing water after heavy rains.
   - **Slope**: As level as possible.
   - **Exposure**: Protected from high winds; Avoid low-lying frost pockets.
   - **Surrounding vegetation**: Few trees; look for problematic plants (i.e. poison ivy, stinging nettles).
   - **Soil**: Test the soil for heavy metals and other contaminants. The University of Vermont, or other regional agricultural extension universities, provides services for soil-testing.

- **Water**: Ideally a close water source is available.
- **Safety**: Site promotes personal safety; If digging, make sure not digging on utility line—Call Before You Dig—811.
- **Accessibility**: Location and layout of site suitable for potential gardener population and for bringing materials onto the site.
- **Size**: Space large enough for the number of potential gardeners, garden infrastructure, a diversity of garden activities, and room for growth.
- **Ownership**: If the potential site is not owned by you or your gardening team, find out who owns the site to see if you can rent or buy the land.

5. Design your garden site (phased development).
   - Conduct a site analysis to determine what your site needs to become a garden and where you should place various features.

What's included in a site analysis?
One way to analyze a site is to map it out and overlay your map of the site with an analysis of physical, programmatic, and design considerations.
- Create a garden site plan that lays out landscape and garden features.
- Divide the site development into multiple phases, as budgeting and time allows.

What features should you consider including in your garden?

6. Develop your garden budget and fundraising plan.
   - Based on your site analysis and site plan, make a list of supplies, materials, and other resources needed.

The author waters her raised bed gardens either early in the morning, or at sundown, in order to let the plants absorb the most water.

- Outline the budget, considering your garden's various developmental stages, from budgeting for garden construction, to ongoing needs, to future development and garden sustainability.
1. Develop a fundraising plan. Consider various fundraising strategies to match your garden's developmental stages, from seeking donated and recycled materials, to conducting bake sales, to writing grants.

2. Build your garden site.
   - Determine a timeline for phased development of your garden site.
   - Gather people together for a garden work party, with an emphasis on party! This is a fun opportunity to bring more people into your garden project and build the community spirit of the garden from the get-go.

From The Vermont Community Garden Network

The author's harvest for the day from one of the productive raised bed gardens on her five-acre parcel of land in Vermont.

HOW TO BUILD A RAISED BED

Notes: The instructions provided are just one way to build a raised garden bed. Many other designs have proven successful. If four-by-four timbers are hard to come by, try using two by eight-inch boards or other sizes that may lower your cost. If you are using thinner boards you can use long screws rather than timber ties, which can be less expensive.

Depending on your gardening needs, you may also want to consider a shorter or higher raised bed design. Hemlock is often used in New England for its longevity, decent price, and availability. Cedar and wood/plastic composite are also options, but can be prohibitively expensive. Due to chemical residue which may impact your organic garden, do not use pressure-treated wood if you are using the beds for food gardens.

Supplies:
- Circular saw and accompanying safety equipment
- Square (tool)
- Level
- Measuring tape
- Pencil
- Shovels
- Hammer
- Scissors
- Wheelbarrow or buckets

Twelve eight-foot four-by-four timbers are needed to assemble a four-layer, four-foot by eight-foot raised bed.

The lumber will be stacked and each layer will overlap the layer below it at the corners. Here are the four different measurements to prepare:

1. First, trim all timbers to the maximum possible common length, as they may not all be exactly eight feet. Set aside four boards. These will be used for the sides of layers 1 and 3.
2. Measure the width of a timber (as it may not be exactly four inches). Double this width and subtract from the length of the timbers cut in step 1. This will be the length to cut the four timbers used for the sides of layers 2 and 4.
3. The end pieces of layers 2 and 4 are made by cutting two timbers in half.
4. Subtract the doubled timber width from the length of the end pieces of layers 2 and 4. This will be the length to cut the two boards used for the ends of layers 1 and 3.

*Note: A simpler option is to cut all the timbers to the maximum possible common length, then cut four timbers in half for the ends and follow the stacking process as outlined below. The bed will end up slightly larger than four feet by eight feet.

The first layer is the most important as all other layers are built on it. The raised bed box will be sturdiest if the first layer is dug into the ground. Use a square and level to ensure that the first layer is as square as possible.

The author's raised bed in Vermont: getting ready to add compost to the soil and plant a row of garlic.

If the area under the raised bed is grass, the sod can be stripped and composted. If the soil underneath the raised bed is determined by a soil test to have contaminants and/or heavy metals, a layer of landscape fabric can be put under the bed as a semi-permeable barrier that excess water in the bed can seep through. When constructing the frame, each layer is nailed to the layer below it with 6-inch long 60d galvanized timber ties, spaced every 16 inches. The final step is to fill the raised beds with a topsoil/compost mix. The beds shown below are 16 feet, 12 feet, and 8 feet long.

FOR ONE 4X8X1' RAISED BED

MATERIALS

Item or Service	# Needed	Unit Sold	Cost/Unit	Total Cost
4 in. x 4 in. x 8 ft. Hemlock lumber	12	Board	$6/board (based on P&P Lumber)	$72
6 in. long 60d galvanized timberties	60	50 piece box or Individually	$30/box or $0.90/tie (based on ACE Hardware)	$39
Topsoil/Compost Mix	39 cubic ft. or 1.43 cubic yd.	Cubic yards (whole units)	$25/1-5 cubic yards (based on Highfields Center for Composting)	$40
Landscape fabric	——————	3 ft. w x 36 ft. l Roll (Recycled Plastic Weed- block)	$21.95/roll (based on Gardener's Supply Co.)	$22
Estimated Total				$173

Harvesting kale and garlic from the author's raised beds.

Chapter 12

SUCCESS STORIES

"The garden is growth and change and that means loss as well as constant new treasures to make up for a few disasters."

—May Sarton

All around the world individuals and municipalities, schools, and universities are starting to compost with enthusiasm and the results are showing that it saves money and helps the environment—a win-win situation to be sure! Where I live, Brattleboro, Vermont, we have one of the first up-and-running municipal composting systems in the country. The local hardware store sells composting bags for now and we hope eventually they will be free. The town solid waste district is also selling the kitchen collector bins and the outside composting collector bin, and the town subsidized some of the cost with money that is expected to be saved on tipping fees by the reduction in heavy household waste.

Vermont will be one of the first states in the country to require municipalities to compost their own household food scraps. Moss Kahler, head of municipal composting in Brattleboro, says there is going to be interest in how the town does as it rolls out the new system.

"Vermont communities are starting to look at this and there is a lot of interest in what we are doing," he said. "People are going to be watching how we do here."

The new Curbside Compost Bins offered for sale, cheaply, by the town of Brattleboro for their highly successful program for homeowners and apartment dwellers to easily compost their kitchen scraps, paper products, cotton, dryer lint, meat scraps, fish, cheese, etc.

MUNICIPAL COMPOSTING IN BRATTLEBORO, VERMONT (MOSS KAHLER)

The town saves fifty-five dollars for every ton of compost that is diverted form the landfill, and another $105 for every ton of recyclable material that stays out of the trash stream.

When the curbside compost program starts, the town will also move toward weekly recycling pickup.

Kahler says studies show that when more people compost it also increases the recycling rate, so Brattleboro is poised to keep tons of trash out of the landfill, as well as save real money on its tipping fees.

Vermont has also passed legislation that will require all municipalities to offer curbside compost and recycling programs, so Kahler said Brattleboro is going to lead the rest of the state in starting its programs.

"It is amazing how the town, and the selectboard have gotten behind this," Kahler said. "The writing is on the wall and more towns are going to have to do this. It is good to be proactive so you don't have to scramble."

The town is asking anyone in Brattleboro who has trash picked up by the town's service to contact the compost coordinator to sign up for the new program.

Kahler says that while recycling is still required in Brattleboro, the compost program will be voluntary.

The three-month pilot program was wildly successful, Kahler said.

Not only did all 153 voluntary participants say that they would continue on with the program, but Kahler said he also received comments that the service was easier and less of a nuisance than some of the participants anticipated.

More than seven hundred households have signed up for the new curbside system and Kahler said he hopes, and expects, to gain another few hundred in the coming months when word gets around about how convenient and effective it is to keep the heavy household solid waste out of the regular trash pail.

There are about 2,700 stops on the town's trash pickup route.

"It's a very good start," Kahler said. "We received a lot of good feedback during the pilot study and I think more people are going to want to take part once we get going."

The town ran a voluntary pilot study of the curbside compost program in the fall with about 150 households taking part.

Kahler said it was largely a complete success and he said the town is now ready to extend to the service to anyone on the regular trash route who wants to take part.

Curbside compost pickup is completely voluntary.

He acknowledges that just about everyone who took part in the pilot study was motivated and committed to making it work; still, participants were surprised at how easy it was and at how much lighter their weekly trash load was, he said.

About 25 percent of the households that took part in the pilot study had never composted before and Kahler says the experience for most part was positive.

Howard Weiss-Tisman, The Brattleboro Reformer

COMPOST EXERCISE ROUTINE

Mavis, the thinnest woman on the block, loves to go out and turn the compost piles in her community garden. She says that using the compost pile as your exercise is so rewarding. It's not a waste.

Her routine goes like this: the community garden has four bins, and gardeners always add to the bin closest to the garden. The instructions to the other gardeners are simple: add to #1 and take compost from #4.

Meanwhile, Mavis-the-compost-maven is taking care of what's happening in the middle. In the spring, as soon as the compost thaws, Mavis forks #3 into #4.

Then she turns #2 into the now-emptied #3, and #1 into the now-emptied #2. As she is turning #1 into #2, she can layer and water as needed. If she runs into a batch of garbage, then she adds a layer of mulch hay or leaves. Then the first bin, the one closest to the plots, is empty again and ready to be filled up during the spring, summer, and fall.

And Mavis feels great! —Cheryl Wilfong

"Zero Waste" in San Francisco, California

According to Zero Waste, San Francisco's city-mandated recycling program has ambitious goals.

Zero waste means products are designed and used according to the waste reduction hierarchy (prevent waste, reduce and reuse first, then recycle and compost) and the principle of highest and best use, so no material goes to landfill or high-temperature destruction.

What prompted San Francisco to push for zero waste?

After San Francisco successfully achieved the state-mandated 50 percent landfill diversion by 2000, San Francisco wanted to extend its commitment to landfill diversion and set a goal of seventy-five diversion by 2010 and zero waste by 2020. Increasing diversion and pursuing zero waste achieves three key sustainability goals:

1. Conserves valuable resources;
2. Reduces environmental impacts, such as climate change and pollution; and
3. Creates green jobs.

When materials are not reused or recycled and sent to the landfill, valuable resources are wasted and greenhouse gasses are emitted into the atmosphere. Compostable materials, like food scraps and yard trimmings that are sent to landfills produce methane, a potent greenhouse gas which is up to seventy-two times more potent than carbon dioxide. San Francisco's Zero Waste program significantly reduces these emissions, making it an essential component in achieving the City's ambitious greenhouse gas reduction goals.

In addition, recycling and composting greatly increase the amount of recyclable materials available to make new products, reducing the need to extract more virgin materials. Food scraps create nutrient-rich compost—a natural fertilizer—to help grow fruits and vegetables in local farms. Compost also helps farms retain water, a precious resource.

San Francisco's zero waste program benefits the economy, as composting and recycling save residents and businesses money and create green jobs.

More Success Stories from *Biocycle*

In the spring of 2014, the town of Bridgewater, Connecticut, began the first curbside collection program for food scraps in the state. Town officials are working with the Housatonic Resources Recovery Authority (HRRA) to operate a program that will provide interested residents with EcoSafe's two-gallon kitchen counter collection bin, six-gallon curbside bin and compostable bags, and an information packet so households can successfully participate in the program. Jen Iannucci, HRRA's Assistant Director, initiated the program and did much of the leg work to make it happen, including surveying residents to gauge interest and developing public education tools, like brochures and website content necessary to support the program.

The City of Austin is expanding its residential food scraps curbside collection pilot. In 2013, nearly two thousand tons of source-separated organics were collected from eight thousand homes as part of the city's pilot project. In February 2014, 6,500 more homes were added, for a total of fourteen thousand homes currently participating.

The city collects food and green waste from residences weekly in ninety-six-gallon carts. Waste eligible for composting is described in outreach materials as "If it grows, it goes!" and includes meat and dairy products. City haulers deliver collected materials to Organics by Gosh, a composting facility in Austin. Contamination has not been a huge issue according to Vidal Maldonado, division manager at Austin Resource Recovery. An audit of all routes indicated a contamination rate of approximately 1 percent, with most coming from plastics and trash, followed by glass. "We don't allow compostable bags or any other bags so that we can see what is going into the bins," says Maldonado. "Our biggest challenge is that participants use the cart just for food waste, instead of mixing it with yard waste. Operationally that is inefficient for us."

The San Diego International Airport has been participating in the City of San Diego's Commercial Food Scraps Composting Program since 2009, diverting an average of sixty tons a year of coffee grounds and fruits. During this time, the airport had one central kitchen and thirty-two food providers managed by HMS Host, which also donated an average of 1,500 pounds of food annually, generating approximately 1,700 meals for food insecure San Diegans. In 2013 the airport completed its major renovation and expansion, adding two new central kitchens managed by High Flying Foods (HFF) and SSP America (SSP). It now offers a total of fifty-seven food vendors that include twelve sit-down restaurants, seventeen fast food eateries, eleven food kiosks, and coffee shops. Twenty-nine of these vendors prepare food at their site. Once construction of the new terminals was concluded, Airport and City staff started working on a logistics plan for the comprehensive food scraps composting program including all foods, and a food donation program.

In February 2014, Synagro Technologies opened a $4.3 million composting facility in Charlotte County, Florida. Synagro worked with local and county officials, the Florida Department of Environmental Protection, and the US EPA to ensure that the plant's development, construction and operation received approval and met all regulatory requirements. The facility will operate under a ten-year lease with the Charlotte County Public Works department.

Missoula, Montana: Carcass Composting Project Protects Bears, Wolves

On many ranches, livestock carcasses are deposited in "boneyards" where they decompose. But when a ranch is near deep wilderness, boneyards may easily attract large carnivores to what seems like a free lunch, as well as increasing the chances of carnivore-human conflict and the risk that the bear or wolf will be put down. To avoid the problem, says Seth Wilson, a biologist for a coalition of ranchers and landowners in Montana called the Blackfoot Challenge—and cofounder of People and Carnivores—ranchers had sent carcasses to the local rendering plant. When that facility closed, the carcasses had to be landfilled, which is costly.

In 2007, Wilson, known as "Dr. Carcass," asked Montana's Department of Transportation (MDT) if it would take some livestock carcasses to the composting facility that MDT had started in Clearwater Junction to handle road-killed wildlife on a trial basis. That experiment evolved into a partnership with MDT, the Montana Fish, Wildlife and Parks Department, US Fish & Wildlife Service (US FWS), and approximately thirty ranches, to compost dead livestock at MDT's predator-resistant central facility. Livestock carcasses from the ranches go into one of ten outdoor bins constructed of Jersey barriers and ground-up asphalt flooring. A five-wire electrical fence surrounds all of the bins and finished compost, which has "taken care of" incursions by wolves or bears, says Bruce Friede, former MDT area supervisor for Upper Blackfoot who has worked with Wilson since the project's inception.

Carcasses are piled onto a twelve-to-eighteen-inch layer of wood chips, covered completely with higher temperature compost. A final layer of ten to fourteen inches of chips helps absorb odor, says Friede. Once the bin is full, MDT waits thirty days before "stirring" the pile. "We have to stir it because the pile is fairly large, and, as the animals are digested, it will shrink," he explains. "We take the loader, back drag [the pile], roll it back into the bin and cover it with wood chips." MDT adds more wood chips to control odors. In drier seasons, the pile is watered for about fifteen minutes twice a day to maintain needed moisture. "If you keep it well-watered, it's very low-odor," notes Wilson. "When we first got started, everyone was like, is this going to be a total mess? But it's pretty contained." After another thirty days, MDT typically unloads the bin and puts the material into a large pile it labels "Done."

MDT has used the compost in various revegetation projects, such as rocky terrain surrounding a new sewer system, says Friede, noting that it got vegetation growing very quickly. "We have done some tests at the Clearwater site, where we put out five or six inches of the compost on some scree, and [the revegetation] was just amazing," adds Wilson. "With everyone contributing, composting costs about $22/per carcass, which is about a third what it would cost to landfill. It's a public-private partnership 365 days a year that has kept cost down and efficiency up."

Sonoma County, California: Worms and Worm Bins For Sale

The Compost Club started in 2003, while Rick Kaye, cofounder, was volunteering as the "recycling coordinator" for his daughter's school in Healdsburg, California. Kaye's mission was to divert organics that the school produced without sending the material offsite. He saw vermicomposting with worm bins as the solution. In its first year, the small,

150-student West Side School converted its twenty pounds of weekly compostable waste into worm castings. Students, teachers, and parents harvested, sifted, bagged, and labeled five-pound bags of vermicompost, then sold them at the Healdsburg Farmers Market. About a half-ton of material was composted; nine hundred dollars was raised for school field trips.

The Compost Club has grown from diverting nine hundred pounds of food scraps in 2003 to 44,000 total pounds diverted in 2013. It now includes fifteen area schools and four regional businesses. The Club relies on grants and donations, and sells its worms and bin systems to the public to sustain the community project. Worms can be purchased for $25/pound. Two sizes of bins (two feet and three feet in diameter and both eighteen inches high) are sold locally. The Healdsburg High Construction and Sustainability Academy constructs the frames. Ordering information can be found at www.compostclub.org.

In late October, entrepreneur Susannah Castle launched Blue Earth Compost, a food waste collection service in Hartford and West Hartford, Connecticut. Castle makes weekly pick-ups at residences and a local juice bar using her VW Jetta wagon. Collected organics are delivered to Harvest New England in Ellington, about twenty miles away. The certified-organic compost produced is periodically "returned" to Castle's customers. For weekly pick-ups, customers pay $8/week, $30/month or $170 for six months. Blue Earth Compost supplies customers with four-gallon bins that each hold up to thirteen pounds of food waste, along with BioBag compostable liners. Castle says that she has found a lot of demand from people interested in recycling their food waste, contrary to

those that believe it is difficult to change behavior in terms of getting folks to separate their organics from the waste stream and properly sort them. "We've audited all of our subscribers at least once and there have been no problems with contamination," Castle adds.

Composting activity is continuing to gain momentum in Connecticut. In the beginning of 2014, state regulations came into effect that require each commercial food wholesaler or distributor, industrial food manufacturer or processor, supermarket, resort, or conference center that generates more than 104 tons of organic waste per year to send that waste to an organic materials recycling facility, pending a permitted facility that is willing to accept the material exists within twenty miles of the generator. In 2020, the law will affect all generators in the above-mentioned categories, regardless of the volume of organic waste that they generate. "With the new recycling mandate, the climate has become more and more encouraging for composting, and there's a lot of buzz around it," notes Castle. After an article about Blue Earth Compost was published in a local newspaper, Castle says she was inundated with calls from prospective customers. The fact that she delivers finished compost to customers has been "a big driver" in stimulating interest.

It has been about three months since Castle began pick ups in a five-square-mile area, and she is now servicing thirty household accounts, the juice bar, and a recycling pilot project at a local grade school. Blue Earth has been adding about three new household residences per week. "We've been ramping up very fast, faster than our projections," Castle adds. "Our capacity is 150 subscribers total. We are small by design. We want to innovate as we scale and grow efficiently."

The Rich Earth Institute in Brattleboro, Vermont, is dedicated to advancing and promoting the use of human waste as a resource. Through research, demonstration, and education projects, they strive to illustrate the positive effect of this approach in important areas including water quality, food security, energy use, soil health, economic sustainability, carbon footprint, public health, and emergency preparedness.

They seek to bring together the knowledge of many disciplines and professions in order to create workable solutions. For this reason, the various perspectives of sanitary engineers, farmers, water quality advocates, businesspeople, agricultural scientists, and regulators are all represented among their board members and collaborators.

The Institute was founded in 2011, and is developing quickly. In 2012 and 2013, they conducted the first controlled field trials in the United States using source-separated human urine as a fertilizer. They envision being involved in the creation of a regional system for recycling source-separated human waste back into agriculture, as well as serving as an intellectual hub for researchers, writers, professionals, and other practitioners who are exploring the intersection of agriculture and sanitation.

More than 170 volunteers in the Brattleboro, Vt., area have contributed urine to the Rich Earth Institute field trials.

Abraham Noe-Hays, research director of the Rich Earth Institute in Vermont, applies urine to a five-by-five-meter test plot on a hay farm.

The author's side garden with bluebird house, flowering annuals and perennials, and fresh compost and mulch. You can do a lot with not much space if you have good organic compost and soil to mix it in. The decaying woodpile from old apple trees in the background is a good source of nutrients to the soil and the author spreads the wood chips around the beds.

Chapter 13

DON'T WORRY! YOUR QUESTIONS ANSWERED

"Garden as though you will live forever."

—William Kent

Why Should I Bother to Compost?

According to the Council of Canada Compost website, there are basically ten reasons who you should love to compost, and in the tradition of the "Top Ten Hits," here they are:

1. **Send less to landfill.** Organics represent over one-third of the materials being sent to landfills. Whether through backyard or large-scale composting or anaerobic digestion, those banana peels, apple cores, and other organic materials can be recycled.
2. **Reduce greenhouse gases.** According to Environment Canada, landfill sites account for about 38 percent of Canada's total methane emissions. It's the organics that are buried in the landfill that are a key contributor to this production of greenhouse gases.
3. **Recover valuable materials.** Composting produces compost, the single most important ingredient for healthy and productive soil.

4. **Decrease soil erosion.** Soil erosion can remove nutrients from the soil, reducing its productivity, as well as reducing runoff that can carry sediment, nutrients and chemicals into waterways thereby creating new sources of pollution. Compost helps enhance soil

A late summer zinnia blooming in the author's raised bed garden.

structure and binds soil particles together.

5. **Revitalize soil.** Compost helps provide sustenance for the very necessary biological diversity in the soil. Plants depend on this to convert materials into plant available nutrients and to keep the soil well-aerated.

6. **Reduce the need to water.** By improving the soil structure through the addition of compost, water is retained and available for plants.

7. **Reduce the need for pesticides.** Compost can help suppress plant diseases.

8. **Save money.** Through backyard composting, you can turn your leftover organics into a valuable soil amendment without spending a dime.

9. **Make your garden grow.** Compost provides essential organic matter for the soil, which is of fundamental importance to its health, vitality, and fertility.

10. **Make a positive environmental difference.** With compost, you can take resources otherwise regarded as waste—organic residuals—and turn them into something of value while at the same time realizing landfill and greenhouse gas reductions, improved soil productivity and water quality.

Will It Improve my Soil?

A healthy, flourishing garden begins with healthy soil. By learning as much as you can about your soil, you will be better able to match plants to your conditions.

You can determine the type of soil you have by conducting a simple test that will reveals its composition (whether it's predominantly clay, loam, or sand), the nutrient levels in your soil and the soil's pH (its acidity or alkalinity).

Scoop a handful of soil and give it a squeeze. If you have sandy soil, it will be crumbly and won't hold its shape in your hand; sandy soils don't retain much moisture. If you have clay soil, it will form a lump when you squeeze it; clay soils get sticky when wet and turn very hard when dry. Loam, the ideal garden soil, will form into a ball when you squeeze it but will break apart easily. To improve any soil—sand, clay, and loam—add compost.

Another way to determine whether your soil is clay, loam, or sand is to put a handful of garden soil in a jar, fill it with water, shake, and then leave it to settle for a day. Sand will settle to the bottom, and silt will be the next layer with clay on top (organic matter will float on the water's surface). Compare the percentage of

Sod roof, above a homemade sauna, on the author's property that needs some soil amendment from compost mixed with topsoil.

each layer to determine whether you've got loam (20 percent clay, 40 percent silt, 40 percent sand), clay (60 percent clay, 30 percent silt, 10 percent sand), or sand (5 percent clay, 10 percent silt, 85 percent sand).

To test the pH levels in your garden—to tell whether your soil's pH is acidic, neutral, or alkaline—a home pH testing kit is available at most nurseries. This will help you determine which plants will do best in your soil conditions.

To determine the drainage capacity of your soil, dig a hole one foot deep and one foot wide. Fill it with water, let it drain completely, then fill again until the soil is saturated. Depending on how long it takes for this last batch to drain, you've either got adequate drainage (less than two hours) or poor drainage (more than two hours).

Whatever your soil type, pH, drainage and nutrient levels, you can improve the health of your soil by adding compost. Dig in lots of compost when first preparing your garden bed for planting. In already established gardens, add a three-inch inch layer of compost around your plants in spring, summer, or fall.

Will Composting Save Water?

Water is a resource too precious to waste. More and more cities are enacting watering bans or restrictions during the summer months when water use increases by 30 to 50 percent. By taking a few simple steps, you can ensure that your green garden conserves water and still looks beautiful.

Enhance the water-retention capability of your garden's soil by digging in compost in spring, summer, or fall. Not only will this organic matter improve your soil's texture and water-retention capabilities, it will also add important nutrients.

Mulch your plants, shrubs, and trees with a three-inch layer of compost, shredded bark, straw, or chopped leaves during the growing season. Make sure the mulch doesn't touch the base of the plant. The mulch layer will conserve moisture in the soil and prevent weeds from sprouting.

When planting young seedlings, create a saucer-like area around the base of the plant so rainwater will be directed to the plant's root zone.

If you live in an area with regular dry periods during the summer months, choose plant drought-tolerant species that thrive with no watering. A local nursery can help you choose drought-tolerant plants, many of which are prolific bloomers—an attractive bonus.

Spaghetti squash in the author's garden.

Place plants with similar moisture needs together in the garden. This way, instead of watering the whole garden indiscriminately, you can water only those plants that need it.

Install a rain barrel, connected to your downspout, so you can collect rain for garden use.

Consider planting native species as these plants are adapted to the climate and rainfall patterns in your region. A great resource for urban action especially is the Chicago Community Climate Action Toolkit. (More info in the Resources.)

How Do I Go Organic with My Home Garden/ Composting System?

For every problem that may arise in your garden, there's a green, organic

A ripe bell pepper in the author's garden.

solution. Instead of using synthetic chemicals, which may leach into and contaminate the soil and groundwater, use these time-tested, organic methods. And remember, the best organic practice is prevention—healthy soil and healthy plants are more resistant to pests and diseases.

Keep your soil healthy by adding lots of organic matter, in the form of compost, throughout the growing season. Compost contributes to the health of the soil by supplying nutrients, improving soil texture and drainage, conserving soil moisture and encouraging earthworms and soil microorganisms.

Keep your plants healthy by making sure they're not too crowded and that they're getting the proper amount of water (neither too much nor too little). Divide overcrowded plants and plant divisions in another spot in your garden or give them to friends.

Hand-pull weeds when they first appear—before they go to seed. By dealing with weeds immediately, you'll save lots of time later.

Inspect your plants regularly, and at the first sign of insect infestation, learn to identify what particular creature is affecting your plant. (Not all bugs are bad! Many are beneficial.)

For a good all-purpose, organic spray to control insects, mix one whole garlic bulb, a generous pinch of cayenne pepper, and **two cups** of water in a blender. Mix thoroughly, let the solids settle, and then pour the liquid into a spray bottle. Spray on the leaves (tops and undersides) and stems of insect-infested plants. You can also use a commercially available organic insecticidal soap, such as Safer's.

Birds eat bugs—celebrate when you see earthworms and birds to your garden.

Research some tips on how certain plantings will attract birds.

Remove diseased plants from the garden and clean your tools regularly.

Consider companion planting in the vegetable garden to keep pests to a minimum. For example, plant marigolds around the tomato patch—the marigolds' strong smell repels insects.

What Is Permaculture and How Can My Compost and Garden Share Space with Wildlife?

The green garden is alive with creatures. Birds, butterflies, and pollinating insects all bring life to the garden and pleasure to the gardener. Hang out the welcome

mat by creating a habitat that meets the needs of wild creatures.

The best way to attract wildlife is to plant a diversity of species: trees, shrubs, and perennials. These different layers in the garden will provide a variety of habitats for the specific needs of various creatures.

Include a variety of flowers that bloom throughout the growing season from spring to fall, ensuring a long-lasting food source for nectar-loving creatures such as butterflies.

Leave seedpods on perennial plants over the winter to provide an important food source for birds. If you have the space, consider planting both deciduous and evergreen trees that will provide year-round habitat for birds.

Choose shrubs that produce berries for birds. A local nursery will be able to suggest appropriate shrubs for your area.

If you have a lawn, consider replacing at least a portion of it with either a flowerbed or a low-growing groundcover. Lawns provide little in the way of wildlife habitat.

Consider adding a water feature to your garden. This is one of the best ways to create wildlife habitat. Your water feature can be as simple as a bowl of water left on the ground in an open area or, better yet, it can be a birdbath. A pond requires more work (both in planning and in maintenance) but has enormous wildlife benefits.

To attract wildlife, it's important to garden organically. Synthetic chemicals kill butterflies and beneficial insects.

Keep a list of the creatures that visit your green garden habitat and share the news of sightings with others in your neighborhood. It may inspire them to create wildlife habitats too.

I Am a Beginner, But How Can I Encourage All This Biodiversity?

Quite simply, biodiversity means the variety of life on earth. Think of it as a web: the more links and strands of connection there are, the stronger the whole web becomes. It's the same for the green garden: with a variety of plants and life forms, the garden as a whole is stronger, healthier, and more resilient.

Biodiversity begins below the ground—a healthy soil teeming with diverse micro-organisms. The best thing you can do to contribute to the life of the soil is to add compost and lots of it. Compost is full of beneficial bacteria and microorganisms that create a healthy, living soil.

Monocultures, such as lawns or the same vegetable crop planted year after year in the same place, are an invitation to infestation! Rotate vegetable crops by planting them in different places within the garden bed each year.

Plant a variety of different species throughout the flower garden, aiming, in particular, for a variety of blooming times, from spring through fall. This way, your biodiverse green garden will meet the needs of a variety of wild creatures—the plant biodiversity will encourage animal biodiversity, too.

Avoid the use of synthetic chemicals in the garden, which destroy good bugs along with bad.

The author's west-side garden with a bluebird house.

Keep a list of all the diverse creatures that visit your green garden—you'll be amazed by the amount of life buzzing in your yard![1]

SUMMER SOLSTICE BONFIRE

Author's note: Cheryl has a very creative approach to her compost pile! The author does not put bones anywhere near her compost pile, cremated or otherwise!

I bought an organic chicken at the Farmers' Market and boiled it up to make chicken soup and chicken salad. But what to do with the skin and bones? You're not supposed to compost them, though my compost is full of chicken bones and spare ribs. I suppose they add a slow-release calcium to the garden. In the winter, I cremate the bones in my wood stove.

But how to dispose of meat bones during the summer? Surely, there's a biodegradable alternative to the trash.

On summer solstice, I have a bonefire. Yes, that's where the word bonfire comes from—burning. . . . Well, maybe we don't want to think too closely about who was being burned. Women. Enemies. Minorities. People who were "different."

[1] The above text is courtesy of Compost Council of Canada, www.compost.org.

In India, still today, dead bodies are cremated in bonfires on platforms along the Ganges River and its tributaries. The ashes are then swept into the holy river, a visible reminder of the cycle of life.

What to do with chicken bones during the summer? Celebrate the summer solstice with a bonfire as the long summer days begin to die in length. —Cheryl Wilfong

Now that My Compost is Producing, What Should I Plant in My Garden?

Native plants are species that existed in an area prior to European settlement. They've developed over millennia and are adapted to local conditions. The big advantage for the green gardener is that native plants tend to be lower maintenance, requiring little in the way of supplementary watering and no synthetic chemicals.

Learn about the native plants that grow in your area as well as which type of habitat they prefer in the wild (for example, woodland, meadow, prairie, wetland). Contact local naturalist groups, gardening organizations, and environmental groups to find out if they've compiled lists of native plants or if they can recommend local wild areas to explore.

Visit a specialty native plant nursery to find out which native plants are commercially available in your area. (Never dig plants from the wild.)

Compare the conditions found in your garden (shade or sun, dry or moist, etc.) to the conditions required by a variety of native plants that you're interested in growing and that are commercially available in your area. The native plants will thrive in your garden when you match the plants to the condition—woodland plants for shade, sun-loving plants for meadows and prairies, wetland plants for moist areas.

Water young transplants for the first six weeks after planting. After that, they should thrive without supplementary watering. Design your native plant garden in whatever style appeals to you—from formal to informal—mandala-shaped gardens are beautiful, or if you are like me, you like the ease of a raised bed.

Now That I Am Composting and Gardening, How Can I Make My Lawn "Greener"?

It is possible to have a healthy lawn without using synthetic chemicals, simply by practicing more sustainable lawn care. The principles are the same as those followed throughout the green garden: maintaining soil health and vitality, watering wisely, and recycling nutrients.

To maintain soil health, top-dress with a fine sprinkling of compost a few times during the growing season.

Lawns require approximately one inch of water a week. If rain doesn't provide enough water, you may need to do some supplementary watering. This should be done in the early morning on a windless day (too much water is lost to evaporation by the sun during the middle of the day or on windy days).

Place a small can by the sprinkler to see how long it takes for an inch of water to accumulate.

The author's native blueberries with compost, organic soil, and mulch applied in the fall.

Set your lawn mower blades at three inches. This is the ideal height for grass to shade out weeds and to keep the soil cool and moist.

Cut no more than a third of the grass height in one cutting and make sure your mower blades are sharp.

Leave grass clippings on the lawn to slowly decompose and return their nutrients to the soil—you can use some to layer your compost pile as well.

A mulching mower/blade will distribute clippings evenly throughout the lawn.

Gently remove thatch buildup in your lawn using a stiff rake. Compost the accumulated debris.

Aerate compacted soil in the spring or fall.

Leave any clover that appears in your lawn—clover fixes nitrogen in the soil and thus improves soil fertility.

Hand pull weeds before they go to seed—this will prevent them from spreading in the garden.

STINKY THOUGHTS

One spring evening, I made my final run to the compost pile at nine and beaned a skunk on the nose with a watermelon rind. I didn't stick around for a closer sighting once I saw that furry white tail start to twitch. When my sweetie came home fifteen minutes later, he said he smelled skunk.

Our thoughts and actions go into a "compost pile" from moment to moment. A thought arises, then it passes. A deed happens, then it's over. Even though it's gone, it leaves the track of its valence. A wholesome thought or deed—of kindness or generosity—lays the path for more wholesome thoughts and deeds. An unwholesome thought or deed lays the pathway for more of the same. In the language of neuroscience, "Neurons that fire together, wire together." In the language of gardeners, "You reap what you sow."

So be careful what you compost. Those stinky thoughts may come back to haunt you. —Cheryl Wilfong

The author doing some weeding and harvesting cherry tomatoes from her garden.

The author's house with solar panels and space to plan more gardens.

Chapter 14

GOING FORWARD

"Adopt the pace of nature: her secret is patience."

—Ralph Waldo Emerson

Without a doubt, composting remains one of the most satisfying and rewarding things I do. My family is involved, too, and my children (now grown), are impressed that most of our waste is now composted, at home and by the town's successful "curbside composting program," and we have very little trash take out to the dump.

When houseguests visit us at our home in Vermont, they sometimes forget about composting, since many of them live around Boston or New York. Usually, I gently remind them that we can put things in the compost bucket in the kitchen.

This humble directive creates a lot of surprise and appreciation for the fact that we are composting and trying to reduce our waste.

Rather than coming down in a condescending way on a houseguest who may not be familiar with composting, I like to talk about the benefits of doing it, and help spread the word. People really seem to appreciate it, and, for some, it may be the very first time they've heard about composting.

Schoolchildren take to it immediately. Since they are more of a *tabula rasa*, in terms of their experience, they love

and appreciate the earth in ways that, as adults, we can easily forget. Sometimes our old habits become ingrained, and we instinctively put the trash right in one container without separating it, without thinking about where it goes. . . . It's almost as if young kids grasp the concept of composting and recycling without a lot of explanation. For them the air, wind, the water, and the dirt in the ground, form part of the natural cycles of the earth, and composting turns into more dirt, with added benefits for their diet.

It's so exciting to see the schools embracing composting! Here in the United States, our culture became obsessed with cleanliness during the early part of the 1990s and into the next decade. Now, however, medical studies show that there are many beneficial bacteria in the world and in our guts, and it might be time to trend away from the antiseptic hand washes, and get our kids out digging in the garden.

My compost pile remains, for me, a thing of beauty. I'll never forget that first year when I was able to use the rich dark humus! As I shoveled it out, I kept exclaiming how great it was, basking in the glow of sunlight as if I wanted the whole world know that I created something magical, something useful, something that would benefit my diet, and something that would return nutrients to what I eat and grow and that I return all that, yet again, to the earth.

So, you see, composting is a cycle. It is a process that involves little skill and brings great joy and rejuvenation to one's life. It is something I can be proud of; it is something tangible, and something I can leave behind.

APPENDIX

This Appendix includes recipes and tips from some master composters, like Cheryl Wilfong, Lars Hundley, and Vern Grubinger. There are many resources out there on the web and other books, all the more reason to celebrate that composting is much more than a fad and is here to stay.

Composting Recipes

These are just some starter recipes. The list of combinations could go on forever. Note that adding too much finished compost to a new batch of compost material may slow composting time some, but it adds a lot of good microorganisms to the mix. Adding a shovel full of your local soil will do the same.

Based on volume and listed in approximate descending order from hottest to least hot mixes:

Recipe #1
2 parts Dry leaves
2 parts Straw or shredded newspaper (black print only)
1 part Manure
1 part Fresh grass clippings
1 part Fresh garden weeds
1 part Food scraps
1 cup Compost starter/activator per 20 lbs of material
1 cup Blood or Alfalfa meal per 20 lbs of material

Recipe #2
3 parts Dry leaves
1 part Fresh grass clippings
1 part Fresh garden weeds
1 part Food scraps
1 cup Compost starter/activator per 20 lbs of material

Recipe #3
6 parts Dry leaves
3 parts Food scraps
3 parts Fresh grass clippings
2 lbs Finished compost and/or 1 cup compost starter/activator per 20 lbs of material

Recipe #4
3 parts Dry leaves
3 parts Fresh grass clippings
2 lbs Finished compost and/or 1 cup compost starter/activator per 20 lbs of material

Recipe #5
3 parts Dry grass clippings
3 parts Fresh grass clippings
1 part Peat moss
1 cup Compost starter/activator per 20 lbs of material
2 lbs Coffee grounds per 20 lbs of material (include filters)

Recipe #6 (experiment more)
4 parts Fresh grass clippings
1 part Peat moss
3 parts Shredded newspaper or cardboard
2 lbs Coffee grounds per 20 lbs of material (include filters)
1 part Food scraps
1 cup Compost starter/activator per 20 lbs of material
1 cup Blood or alfalfa meal per 20 lbs of material

Knowing Your Soil pH is Important

The pH of your soil is important to know as it should influence what you put in your compost mix. The term pH describes the alkalinity (sweetness) or acidity (sourness) of soil or compost. The pH scale runs from one (indicating pure acidity) to fourteen (which is purely alkaline). Something neutral would be a seven. Most plants like, and microorganism operate best in, a pH median between six and seven. Average garden soils range from five to seven. A swamp peat is around three, arid desert soils range from nine to eleven and pure water is seven.

There are many ways of testing for the pH of your soil. One way is to dig a hole in your yard two to four inches deep and clean out twigs and debris, then fill it with distilled water. After you let it sit for a while. It should be muddy. With a pH test probe, you then hold it in place for sixty seconds.

The pH is measured on a scale of one to fourteen and a measurement of seven is neutral soil; above is too alkaline and below is too acidic. It is a good idea to take several measurements from around the yard and then take an average. According to Organic Gardening, one of the best deals for gardeners is a soil test, available through local cooperative extension offices or private laboratories.

Health and Safety Guidelines

There are two potential hazards in working with compost. The first concerns the materials used in composting that could contain disease-causing organisms or pathogens. For example this is why it is best to avoid meat, dairy products, and the other materials listed as not recommended. While not a widespread problem, the second concern relates to allergic reactions to airborne spores. Here are some specific points from Cornell University's Guidelines for Prudent Composting:

1. Avoid certain inputs to the compost pile such as raw poultry or meat wastes and plate scrapings from people who are ill.
2. Consider managing your composting system to ensure that it gets and stays hot long enough to reduce pathogens.
3. Practice good personal hygiene when handling compost. Proper personal sanitation is the most effective method for controlling the impact of any pathogens that may be in the compost. Wash hands after handling compost and/or use gloves. If the compost is particularly dusty, watering is an option.
4. Persons with weakened immune systems or medical conditions that compromise the body's ability to fight infection should use caution when handling compost.
5. If possible, allow composts that are produced in a small-scale setting to age for at least a year before use.

Composting Leaves

This information is from the useful website, *The Compost Guide*, by Lars Hundley (see Resources for more information). Some people complain to us that they have no luck composting leaves. "We make a pile of our leaves," these people say, "but they never break down." That is indeed a common complaint.

There are two things you can do that will guarantee success in composing leaves:

1. Add extra nitrogen to your leaf compost. Manure is the best nitrogen

supplement, and a mixture of five parts leaves to one part manure will certainly break down quickly. If you don't have manure—and many gardeners don't—nitrogen supplements like dried blood, cottonseed meal, bone meal, and Agrinite will work almost as well. Nitrogen is the one factor that starts compost heap heating up, and leaves certainly don't contain enough nitrogen to provide sufficient food for bacteria. Here is a rough guide for nitrogen supplementing: add two cups of dried blood or other natural nitrogen supplement to each wheelbarrow load of leaves.

2. The second thing to do to guarantee leaf-composting success is to grind or shred your leaves. We will deal with this in detail later on, but let me tell you right now that it will make things simpler for you in the long run. A compost pile made of shredded material is really fun to work with, because it is so easily controlled and so easy to handle.

3. A compost pile can be made in almost any size, but most people like to make rectangular-shaped piles, because they are easier to handle. It is a good idea to put the material in the heap of layers. Start with a six-inch layer of leaves, either shredded or not shredded. Then add a two-inch layer of other organic material that is higher in nitrogen than leaves. Try to pick something from this list: manure, garbage, green weeds, grass clippings, or old vines from your garden. You can add low-nitrogen things like sawdust, straw, ground corn cobs, or dry weeds if you put in a nitrogen supplement such as described above. It is important to mix leaves from packing down in a dry mat. Keep the heap moist, but not soggy.

Turn the heap every three weeks or sooner if you feel up to it. If you can turn it three or four times before late spring

comes, you will have fine compost ready for spring planting use.

You can make compost out of leaves in as little time as fourteen days by doing these things:

1. Shred or grind the leaves.
2. Mix four parts ground leaves with one part manure or other material liberally supplemented with nitrogen.
3. Turn the heap every three days. Turning a heap made of shredded leaves is not difficult because the compost is light and fluffy.

One more tip: why not experiment with covering your heap with a plastic sheet? It will keep in the warmth and prevent the heap from getting too wet or too dry.

Potting Mixes for Organic Gardeners

Vern Grubinger, vegetable and berry specialist
University of Vermont Extension

Soilless potting mixes have long been used for greenhouse production of bedding plants, vegetable transplants, and container-grown ornamentals. By avoiding the use of topsoil, the risk of pathogenic microorganisms in this media may be reduced, avoiding problems with diseases like damping-off. In addition, topsoil is relatively heavy and dense so it can contribute to poor aeration and drainage in a potting mix. Soilless mixes should be formulated to have optimal physical and chemical properties that promote germination and healthy seedling growth.

Qualities of a good mix. Poor performance in a potting mix is costly, since greenhouse space is expensive and so is having to toss out some seedlings or replant entirely. Optimal mix characteristics include the right density and porosity to provide good aeration and also good water holding capacity; proper pH; enough available nutrients to get plants off to a good start; and the absence of excess salts and plant pathogens. On organic farms, the mix must not contain any prohibited ingredients.

Organic vs. conventional mixes. Generally speaking, all soilless potting mixes contain a 'base' ingredient, usually sphagnum peat, or sometimes coir. These provide a good physical environment for root growth but are relatively inert in terms of nutrient content and biological activity. Other materials may be added to improve drainage, adjust density, and/or alter water holding capacity, such as perlite, vermiculite, or builder's sand. Ground limestone may be needed to raise the pH. Fertilizers are added to provide available nutrients and obviously that's where conventional and organic mixes differ. In addition, organic mixes typically contain mature compost to provide slow release nutrients and contribute to good physical and biological conditions for plant growth, whereas conventional mixes rarely contain compost.

Issues with compost in potting mix. In some ways, compost is like snowflakes—no two batches of compost are exactly alike. So while compost usually adds value to a potting mix, it can also add a measure of uncertainty about performance that is not the case with conventional mixes. Immature compost in particular can harm seedlings by releasing ammonia, or tying up nitrogen, or stunting growth because of organic acids that have not fully decomposed. To avoid these problems it is important to use only mature compost, and to buy it from a reputable source or to carefully make your own using a consistent supply of high quality ingredients.

It's a good idea to keep organic potting mixes warm and moist for a week or two before planting with them. That allows microbial activity to kick in, and can reduce potential potting mix problems by allowing excess ammonium or organic acids to dissipate.

Compost is rarely used by itself as a potting medium. Compost alone does not have the optimal water holding characteristics, and soluble salt levels may be higher than optimal for potting mix. Plus, high quality compost can be relatively expensive so it makes sense to dilute it with other ingredients like peat. Organic potting mixes are typically made with 20 percent to 50 percent compost by volume, depending on the type of crop that will be grown in the mix, the container size, and the growing conditions.

Common potting mix ingredients. Sphagnum peat moss is a stable organic material that holds fifteen to thirty times its weight in water and decomposes very slowly. It contains about 1 percent nitrogen, but little is released because it breaks down so slowly. It has a pH of about four so lime must be added to the mix to along with sphagnum peat, at the rate of 8.5 lb. per cubic yard of peat to neutralize the acidity.

Coir comes from coconut husks and is a waste product of the coco fiber industry. It has physical properties much like peat but a higher pH of about six. It holds up to nine times its weight in water. It can have a high salt content.

Limestone is either calcitic (high calcium) or dolomitic (high magnesium; both are used to increase the pH of a mix but dolomite is preferable for supplying both Ca and Mg.

Vermiculite helps hold water and fertilizer in the potting mix, and it also contains some calcium and magnesium. It has a pH near neutral. Vermiculite comes in different grades; medium grade is usually used for starting seeds, a coarse grade may be used for larger plants.

Perlite is a volcanic rock that has been heated and expanded. It is lightweight, sterile, and has a neutral pH. It can be used to improve reduce the weight of a potting mix and increase its aeration and drainage.

Coarse washed sand, also called builder's sand, can be used to add air space to the potting mix and increase its weight. It has a neutral pH and provides almost no fertility to plants. Sand may be used when added weight is needed for growing tall or top heavy plants that might fall over if grown in a lightweight mix.

Fertilizers for organic mixes. In some cases, compost can provide adequate amounts of nutrients for transplant production but usually some fertilizer is added to the mix, especially if larger plants are to be produced or if small cell sizes are used that will require relatively high levels of available nutrients in order to sustain plant growth over time. Common organic fertilizers to provide phosphorus include bone meal, bone char, or rock phosphate; potassium can be provided by potassium sulfate, sul-po-mag or greensand; magnesium can come from epsom salts or sul-po-mag. In some cases a blended fertilizer may be used, such as pelletized chicken manure compost but such materials are usually reserved for field use rather than potting mix due to their slower nutrient availability.

Nitrogen availability. Assuring sufficient nitrogen in a form plants can use is often a concern with organic potting mix formulations, as nitrogen release may be quite variable depending on the compost that's used and the extent to which it is source of nitrogen. Most organic potting mixes are supplemented with fertilizers: sources such as blood meal, crab meal, fish meal, or plant meals like alfalfa or soybean provide additional nitrogen to feed plants for several weeks or months. Note that Chilean nitrate is expected to be prohibited for use in organic production sometime in 2012.

Some growers water with fish emulsion or other soluble organic nitrogen fertilizers to keep their transplants 'growing on' if a mix has run out of available nitrogen. Re-potting some plants, like tomato seedlings, into fresh mix is another way to keep them growing well.

When using blood meal, partially composted manure or poultry-manure-based fertilizer, be aware that these high-in-nitrogen sources need some time to allow for microbial activity start breaking the organic forms of nitrogen and drive them to nitrate (the process called mineralization). If used for planting too soon, when first wetted and just starting to break down, these materials may give off ammonia, organic acids, and other compounds that can damage germinating seeds and young plants. It is best to moisten the potting mix at least a week or two before you plant into it, making sure it stays warm and allowing time for phytotoxic compounds to dissipate.

Many things can lead to poor germination, including a mix with excess salts, improper pH, unfinished compost, or nutrient imbalances. Old seeds, improper watering, and root disease can also be to blame.

Avoiding performance problems. While many growers have had success with compost-based potting mixes, the performance of such mixes, whether commercially produced or homemade, has sometimes been inconsistent. In the worst cases, growers have experienced significant financial loss due to poor seedling growth associated with a problem mix. Poor seedling growth in compost-based mixes can result from low levels of available nutrients, high levels of soluble salts, excessive density of the mix, and/or the lingering presence of the harmful byproducts of initial decomposition mentioned above. In some cases the problem is not due to the mix but to management issues, like cold temperatures, improper watering, or root disease.

Test your mix. It is a very good idea to test your organic potting mix well in advance of using it. Send a sample to a soil test lab at a land grant university or at a private company that specializes in horticulture. Do not request a regular field soil test, since potting mixes differ from field soil; they are much higher in organic matter and usually much higher in available nutrient content. A potting soil test will also measure soluble salts (electrical conductivity) and nitrogen in the nitrate and ammonium forms, which a field soil test doesn't measure.

Growers should use the low-cost saturated media extract test (also called greenhouse media test), to get data on the pH, soluble salt, and nutrient levels of their potting mix well in advance of planting. Here are the results of one sample.

The soil test to use for potting mixes is the saturated media extract (SME), also called a greenhouse media test or soilless media test. Unlike field soil tests that extract nutrients with weak acid solutions, the SME sample is mixed with distilled water at a standard dilution and then analyzed. Since different labs may use different dilutions, stick with one lab. To get an accurate reading, be sure that the potting mix has been moist and warm for at least a week prior to sampling. Most labs require a pint of mix to work with, and turnaround time is similar

to a regular soil test: a week or two. It's a good idea to test each batch of potting mix, and to be able to compare results from mixes that performed well to those that didn't. The cost is low, about fifteen or twenty dollars per SME sample.

'Bioassays' are another way to test the quality of a potting mix. All you have to do is sow some fast-growing crops in the mix several weeks before you plan to use it. Cress, oats, and beans are just a few to consider. Some growers also like to test their mixes with slower-growing crops. Onions can be useful for bioassays as they seem to require a very high quality mix for good germination and growth. It makes sense to include any key crops that you grow as part of your bioassay.

Compare potting mixes. Without a side-by-side trial, it's hard to evaluate the relative performance of your current potting mix. So even if you have one you like, plant a few trays of the same seeds using another potting mix brand or recipe. It may surprise you to see how poorly your plants do next to a different formulation.

If things go wrong. Go ahead and submit sample(s) for SME testing; better late than never. Having this data in hand is part of the process of elimination to identify the problem. Is the pH off? Are soluble salts too high? Is there sufficient available nitrogen for plant growth? Once you have that data in hand, contact your potting mix supplier and ask if others growers have reported problems. A good supplier will appreciate communication from their customers, and be able to provide technical advice.

"Buying potting mix from a company like ours means you are buying into a network of organic growers" says Karl Hammer, owner of Vermont Compost Company. "That has great value for both buyers and sellers of the product. Sometimes I get a

call about a problem but when I follow up with other growers using the same mix to grow the same crops, I find that they have no issues. Then it's probably related to a greenhouse management practice. In fact, 90 percent of the problems I see have to do with overwatering in short daylight and cold weather conditions.

Overwatering cools the growing medium, reducing microbial activity and root growth, and it can leach out available nutrients. It's much better to keep your growing medium on the dry side, and if possible, provide bottom heat. Over-the-top watering by hand with cold water creates a lot of plant growth problems in organic potting mixes."

Photo by Meghan Kanady

Well-made compost piles contain enough porous material like leaves or straw to promote passive aeration; since these materials are high in carbon, sufficient high-nitrogen ingredients like manures are also needed to stimulate microbial activity. (Note: Greenmarket collections do not accept manure, but food scraps provide plenty of nitrogen!)

GLOSSARY

Acid: A substance with pH between zero and seven.

Actinomycetes: Decomposer organisms that are part bacteria and part fungus, with a grayish cobwebby look. Actinomycetes live in medium temperatures in backyard compost. Actinomycetes break down woody, carbon-rich material and give finished compost its sweet, earthy smell.

Aeration: A way of allowing air to get into compost.

Aerobic: With oxygen. Decomposer organisms that require oxygen to carry out their life functions will produce sweet, earthy-smelling compost.

Anaerobic: Without oxygen. Anaerobic conditions breed decomposer organisms that live in the absence of oxygen and give off rotten-smelling odors.

Bacteria: A group of microorganisms primarily responsible for decomposition in a backyard compost bin. Also present in worm composting systems.

Bedding: Material such as dead leaves or shredded paper used to retain moisture, create air space, and cover food scraps in a worm composting system.

Biodegradable: Any material that can be broken down into smaller components by the biological processes of digestion and decomposition.

Carbon: A basic element found in compostable material. Materials high in carbon should be mixed with materials high in nitrogen to provide the microorganisms an optimal balance of thirty parts carbon to one part nitrogen (or fifty/fifty by volume). Materials high in carbon are usually brown, dry, and woody; some examples include twigs, dead leaves, straw, newspaper, or sawdust.

Cocoon: Egg cases in which red worms lay their eggs. These egg cases usually hatch two to three baby worms.

Compost: The end result of living organisms digesting and reducing organic material into a dark, rich, earthy-smelling soil amendment. The process is called composting.

Decomposers: Organisms that feed primarily on dead organic material, reducing and digesting it into humus.

Decomposition: The process of materials being digested and broken down into simpler substances, making nutrients more available to plants. Decomposition happens all the time in nature and in human-managed systems such as compost piles.

Energy Flow Cycle: The movement of the sun's energy through an ecosystem. Plants convert the sun's energy into food through photosynthesis. Animals consume the plants. Decomposers eat the dead animals and plants, retuning nutrients that plants need to grow back to the soil.

Erosion: The loss of humus and topsoil through the movement of water, wind, or animals. Compost can help replace lost topsoil. Mulches protect topsoil from being lost to erosion.

Food Scraps: Food that can be put in a compost pile, typically fruit and vegetable scraps. To avoid attracting pests, meat, dairy, and oils should not be composted.

Fungus: A group of decomposer organisms, commonly found in compost piles, which break down organic material into humus.

Humus: The result of organic material being decomposed into a complex, highly-stable material containing plant nutrients. Humus is formed in nature and in managed systems like compost piles.

Landfill: A place where solid waste is buried in the ground. Modern landfills have clay bottoms and a liner, as well as leachate and gas collection systems. Solid waste needs to be covered daily with soil or other material. Many landfills are reaching capacity.

Leachate: Liquid that has passed through solid material and has soluble materials suspended in it. Leachate from landfills can be hazardous and can leak into groundwater supplies.

Macroorganisms: Organisms that are visible to the naked eye, such as worms, sow bugs, and beetles.

Microorganisms: Organisms too small to be seen with the naked eye, such as bacteria and some fungi.

Mulch: Material placed on top of garden beds or around plants. Mulches help deter weeds, hold water, and stop erosion. Shredded or decomposed organic matter makes excellent mulch.

Nitrogen: An element found in compostable material. Materials high in nitrogen should be mixed with materials high in carbon to give the microorganisms a balanced diet of thirty parts carbon to one part nitrogen (or fifty/fifty by volume). Materials high in nitrogen are usually wet and green; some examples include manures, fresh plant clippings, and food scraps.

Nutrient Cycle: The movement of nutrients cycling from living plants, to animals, to decomposers, and returned to the earth in the form of humus.

Organic: Any material that was once living, or material produced by a living organism. "Organic" may also be used to describe food grown using sustainable agriculture methods.

Red Worms: The type of earthworm typically used in worm composting systems. Red worms can be found in leaf mold and manure piles and can be bought in bait shops and gardening stores. Their Latin (scientific) name is *Eisena foetida.*

Topsoil: The soil on the surface that accumulates humus and organic matter.

Vericompost: Compost produced using red worms.

Worm Castings: Worm manure. This high quality soil amendment is the final product from worm composting and can be used as a rich soil amendment.

Worm Bin: The container in which worms, bedding, and composting food waste are kept.

RESOURCES

Vermont Compost Company

Vermont Compost Company was founded by organic crop growing professionals to meet the need for high quality composts and compost-based living soil mixes for certified organic plant production. They are committed to solving the sometimes difficult problems of producing vigorous plants in containers by organic methods. They make their blended soils from ingredients selected with the benefit of many years of experience in protecting their farms from contamination.

Vermont Compost Company
1996 Main Street
Montpelier, VT 05602
http://vermontcompost.com

Highfields Center for Composting

The mission at Highfields, now closed, was to close the loop on community-based, sustainable food and agricultural systems, thus addressing soil health, water quality, solid waste, farm viability, and climate change. They researched, educated, and provided technical services for composting and comprehensive food waste recycling programs.
http://highfieldscomposting.org

Books and Publications:

Here is a bibliography of sorts, of books that have influenced Karl Hammer's philosophical and practical approach to his life and business at Vermont Compost.

Agriculture, by Rudolf Steiner
An Agricultural Testament, by Sir Albert Howard
Chicken Man, by Michelle Edwards
Empty Shells, by Thea Lowry
Farmers of Forty Centuries: Permanent Agriculture in China, Korea and Japan by F.H. King
Media and Mixes for Container-Grown Plants, by A.C. Bunt
Out of the Earth: Civilization and the Life of the Soil, by Daniel Hillel
Physics of Agriculture by F.H. King
Sherry and the Sherry Bodegas, by Jan Read
Soil & Civilization, by Edward Hyams
Soil management: Compost Production and Use in Tropical and Subtropical Environments, by H.W. Dalzell, A.J. Biddlestone, K.R. Gray, and K. Thurairajan
Soil Microorganisms and Higher Plants, by N.A. Krasil'nikov
Soils and Men: Yearbook of Agriculture 1938, by the United States Department of Agriculture
Starting Early Vegetable and Flowering Plants Under Glass, by Charles H. Nissley

Backyard Composting by Harmonious Technologies
Composting In The Class Room by Nancy Trautmann & Marianne Krasny of Cornell University
How to Compost: Everything You Need to Know to Start Composting, and Nothing You Don't! by Lars Hundley
Let it Rot! by Stu Campbell
The Meditative Gardener: Cultivating Mindfulness of Body, Feelings, and Mind, by Cheryl Wilfong, www.meditativegardener.com

Composting Across the Curriculum

Marin County Department of Solid Waste, "Do the Rot Thing." This guide was originally published in July 1997 by the Alameda County Waste Management Authority & Source Reduction and Recycling Board, San Leandro, California, and permission to copy the materials was freely given in the original booklet. This guide was reproduced and republished for access via the Internet by the Central Vermont Solid Waste Management District, Montpelier, Vermont, in January 2007.

Useful Websites

Worms

http://downtoearthwormfarmvt.com/worm-farm

Down to Earth Worm Farm of VT is an indoor vermicomposting facility, where you'll find large drawers full of red wiggler composting worms. They are fed compostables, i.e., kitchen scraps, coffee grounds, garden waste, manure, leaves, etc. In turn, they render worm castings (worm poop), which is the best natural plant food and soil revitalizer. The castings are harvested and packaged for sale to gardeners and houseplant lovers.

www.organicnation.tv

Kids and Composting

EnviroMom.com

EnviroMom.com launched in March 2007. It is a site for anyone who wants to live lightly on the planet. Heather Hawkins and Renee Limon are the co-founders of this group. Heather and Renee are stay-at-home moms, best friends, and neighbors who met in the Hillsdale neighborhood of southwest Portland. They each have two children who happen to be the same ages (nine and six) and attended the same schools. Renee and Heather both completed the Master Recycler course offered through Portland's regional government, which gave them a greater understanding of Reduce/Reuse/Recycle and how their choices and actions impact the natural environment. When they launched EnviroMom in March 2007, they formed their first GreenGroup—a group of moms who meet monthly and exchange ideas on green living with children. They are trying to raise their kids to care about the environment and manage healthy households.

KidsGardening.org

KidsGardening.org is a resource of the National Gardening Association. Check it out for lots of great ideas for gardening with kids. www.kidsgardening.org.

Compost Bin Plans

The most beautiful and practical compost bin ever!

For an introduction to why and how the compost bin made from these particular compost bin plans works so well, please visit homemade compost bin.

www.vegetable-gardening-with-lorraine.com/compost-bin-plans.html

The Author's New Greenhouse Information

Growing year-round in northern climates requires protection from the elements. Ever-Green Houses provide a rugged, weather-proof environment for year-round growing with heavy-duty, and self-assembly, 2x6 construction, which protects against wind and snow.

Website: www.ever-greenhouses.com
Contact: info@ever-greenhouses.com

Additional Online Resources

Chalker-Scott, Linda. Washington State University, "The Myth of Compost Tea, Episode III: "Aerobically-brewed compost tea suppresses disease." http://puyallup.wsu.edu/~linda chalker-scott/horticultural myths_files/Myths/Compost tea 3rd time.pdf.

Cournoyer, Caroline. Governing: The States and Localities, "Curbside Composting Added to a Major City: Is It Yours?." Last modified February 2012. www.governing.com/topics/energy-env/gov-curbside-composting-added-to-major-city.html.

Full Cycle, "Vermiculture" www.fullcycle.co.za/index.php/Information/more-information.html.

Grover, Sami. TreeHugger, "How to Make Compost Tea & Why You Should." Last modified February 04, 2011. www.treehugger.com/lawn-garden/how-to-make-compost-tea-why-you-should.html.

Halepis, Harriette. Mother Nature Network, "The ultimate urban composting guide." Last modified September 30, 2010. www.mnn.com/your-home/at-home/stories/the-ultimate-urban-composting-guide.

Hundley, Lars. *How to Compost: Everything You Need to Know to Start Composting, and Nothing You Don't!* Amazon Digital Services, 2012.

Hundley, Lars. "Compost Guide: Tips for Home Composting." http://compostguide.

com/.Ibiblio.org. "Class Summary, Organic Gardening." http://ibiblio.org/rge/course/

Louisiana.gov. "Did you know… Earthworms." http://deq.louisiana.gov/portal/Portals/0/assistance/educate/DYK-earthworms.pdf.

North Coast Gardening, "Gardening Basics: How to Amend Soil." http://www.northcoastgardening.com/2009/06/organic-gardening-101-soil/

Organic Gardening. "How to Brew Compost Tea." www.organicgardening.com/learn-and-grow/compost-tea.

Priebe, Maryruth Belsey. EcoLife, „Urban Composting Overview." www.ecolife.com/garden/composting/how-to-urban-compost.html.

Seattle Tilth, "Composting Chicken Manure." http://seattletilth.org/learn/resources-1/city-chickens/compostingchickenmanure

University of Florida. "How to Use Compost." http://sarasota.ifas.ufl.edu/compost-info/tutorial/how-to-use-compost.shtml.

University of Illinois Extension. "Composting for the Homeowner." http://web.extension.illinois.edu/homecompost/benefits.cfm.

UPenn, "Earthworms" www.sas.upenn.edu/~rlenet/Earthworms.html.

Vegetable Gardening with Lorraine. www.vegetable-gardening-with-lorraine.com.

Vermont Community Garden Network, The. http://vcgn.org/garden-organizer-toolkit/coordinating-tools/start-a-garden/

WikiHow, "How to Use Your Compost." www.wikihow.com/Use-Your-Compost.

STILL HUNGRY FOR MORE INFO? CHECK OUT THESE GREAT SITES, TOO!

http://compostingcouncil.org/index.cfm (US Composting Council)

http://csanr.wsu.edu/compost (Washington State University Compost Connection)

http://sarasota.ifas.ufl.edu/compost-info/tutorial/quick-tutorial.shtml (University of Florida Composting Center)

www.biodynamics.com/content/biodynamic-compost-preparations

www.cfe.cornell.edu/compost/Composting_homepage.html (Cornell Composting)

www.compost.org (the Compost Council of Canada)

www.cornell.edu

www.deeproot.com/blog/blog-entries/what-is-compost

www.epa.gov

www.epa.gov/compost (US Environmental Protection Agency Composting)

www.gardenweb.com

www.motherearthnews.com

www.organicgardening.com

www.recycle.cc (Recycling and Composting Online)

Live on the west coast? Check out these compost education and resources specifically for Western agriculture

www.2.aste.usu.edu/compost/

www.ithaca.edu/staff/mdarling/Composting.htm

www.epa.gov/osw/conserve/pubs/food6.pdf

http://eartheasy.com/grow_compost.html#a

nyc compost project tip sheet
get all the dirt at www.nyc.gov/wasteless/compost
Funded by the NYC Department of Sanitation, Bureau of Waste Prevention, Reuse & Recycling

The NYC Compost Project runs many innovative programs to encourage composting in all five boroughs. Funded and managed by the Department of Sanitation's Bureau of Waste Prevention, Reuse and Recycling, each NYC Compost Project location offers home composting demonstrations, a compost helpline, and a variety of compost-related workshops and classes.

For recycling and waste prevention info, call 311 or visit www.nyc.gov/wasteless

Build a 3-Bin Compost System

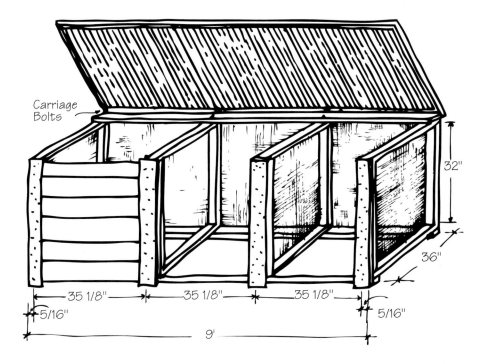

Carriage Bolts

32"

36"

35 1/8"   35 1/8"   35 1/8"

5/16"   5/16"

9'

Materials
7 – 12' cedar 2x4s
3 – 8' cedar 2x2s
1 – 12' cedar 2x6
5 – 12' cedar 1x6s
31' of 36" wide 1/2" hardware cloth
12 – 1/2" carriage bolts, 4" long
12 washers and 12 nuts for bolts
2 lbs of 3 1/2" galvanized screws
200 poultry wire staples

Tools
Handsaw or circular power saw
Drill/driver with 1/2" and 1/8" bits
Hammer
Tin snips
Tape measure
Pencil
3/4" socket or open ended wrench
Carpenter's square or T-square
Safety glasses, ear protection, and dust mask

♻ Save for reference—or recycle it!
6/09

(continued)

nyc compost project tip sheet

get all the dirt at www.nyc.gov/wasteless/compost

Funded by the NYC Department of Sanitation, Bureau of Waste Prevention, Reuse & Recycling

---

Construction Instructions

Build dividers & end sections (Use 2x4s)

- From the 2x4s, cut **eight 32" pieces** for the vertical uprights.
- From the 2x4s, cut **eight 36" pieces** for the horizontal connectors.
- Butt 2 vertical uprights between 2 horizontal connectors to form a frame. Mark and pre-drill the holes. Use screws to secure. Check frame for squareness.
- Make a total of four frames.
- Cut four 35" long sections of hardware cloth.
- Clip extra wire off ends.

- Stretch the hardware cloth across each frame. Attach the screen tightly into place with poultry staples hammered in every 4" around the edge (36" width of cloth is attached to 36" horizontal connectors).

Set up dividers and attach bottom baseboards and top support (Use three 2x4s)

- From the 2x4s, **cut three 9' lengths** to create 2 baseboards and a top support.
- On the side of the boards, mark 36" in from each end.
- On each divider, measure and mark centers on both ends of the 36" pieces (top and bottom horizontal connectors).
- Stand the dividers parallel to one another and 36" apart.
- Place one 9' baseboard on top of the dividers.
- Position the baseboard flush against the outer edges of the end dividers.
- Line up center lines of middle dividers with marks on the baseboard.
- Use a screw to temporarily hold the baseboard to each divider.
- Drill a 1/2" hole through each junction, centered 1" in from the inside edge of baseboard and 1" from inside edge of divider upright.
- Insert carriage bolts from the baseboard side through the divider. Secure with washers and nuts but do not tighten yet.
- Place second 9' baseboard on top of the dividers and repeat process for attaching it.
- Turn the unit right side up and attach 9' top support in the same manner as baseboards (the board will be at the back of the bin).
- Use the carpenter's square or measure between opposite corners to make sure the bin is square.
- Check that the dividers and end sections are at a 90° angle to the top board. Tighten all top support bolts securely.
- Turn bin over and check to make sure bin is square, and dividers and end sections are positioned properly. Tighten all baseboard bolts securely.

Attach hardware cloth

- Using scrap from 2x4s, cut two 28-$^{1}/_{2}$" pieces to insert in gap between the baseboards along the end sections of bin. (Measure gap before cutting scraps.)
- Insert scraps and screw into place on the bottom of the bin.
- Fasten a 9' long piece of hardware cloth securely to the bottom of the bin with poultry staples every 4" around the frame.
- Attach a 9' long piece of hardware cloth to the back of the bin.

Front and back runners for slats (use 2x6s and 2x2s)

- From 2x6s, **cut four 36" pieces** for front runners.
- Center the boards on the front of the dividers, flush with the top edge, and screw in securely.

- From 2x2s, **cut six 34" pieces** for back runners.
- Attach the back runners on insides of divider. Back runners should be parallel to front runners and set back 1" (the gap will hold the slats).

Slats (use 1x6s)

- From 1x6s, **cut eighteen 31" pieces** for front slats. (Measure clearance before cutting and test 1st slat before cutting the rest.)

ACKNOWLEDGMENTS

The book was an evolution into itself, and there are many people to thank for making it possible. First and foremost, I want to thank my editor, Abigail Gehring, who believed in this project from the beginning, and was its champion. Being a beginning composter myself, I was able to write a book from that perspective, and Abigail was the development editor who saw the need for such a book. It is with much gratitude toward her that I write this now, looking out my office window at the simple wooden compost that stands at the edge of my back yard—nearby sits my "Darth Vadar" composter that is full of decaying dry brown leaves that I use for layers—a perfect symbiosis to this scene, at least to my eye.

The publishing house of Skyhorse in New York City is in the forefront, publishing books about meaningful topics that make a difference in the world, and for that I am proud to say I am a Skyhorse author. I'd like to thank Tony Lyons, and the staff at Skyhorse for making a beautiful book, and believing in it as well.

Since no book is ever made in isolation, there is someone else I'd really like to extend my gratitude toward, the author of the foreword and many of the sidebars that grace the book's pages, Cheryl Wilfong. I first met Cheryl when I worked on her second book, *The Meditative Gardener*. I have to admit, I was a bit intimidated before I met her because she is well known in southern Vermont as a master gardener and one of the founders of the Insight Meditation Group in Brattleboro. But once we met and began spending time together, I found her to be one of the most generous and supportive people I know. She is also a master com-

poster! When I started working on *The Organic Composting Handbook*, I felt like it needed "something to make it different"; something fun to read on a winter's night when you are dreaming about the garden you will endeavor to plant in the spring. Here, in Vermont, we get a lot of snow, so many of us spend long hours at home dreaming of gardens. That special touch came in the form of Cheryl's whimsical and touching "sidebar text stories" that I asked her to write. I wrote a few also, and we began to go back and forth via email, and each time she sent me a new one, I delighted in their subjects and how they related to composting! From the Buddhist perspective of the death of a loved one with the cycle of rebirth in the art of composting, to finding a Christmas decoration at the bottom of the pile, to dealing with critters and burning bones, Cheryl "says it all." I am delighted to share the spotlight with my dear friend and fellow avid composter!

There are many others I'd like to thank: First, my husband, Steve Carmichael, who built our house himself (with the help of a great crew) using locally-sourced lumber and even had cabinet timbers cut and milled from our property with a portable saw mill. It was Steve who helped me build the "best composter ever," the one I describe in the book. His patience in supporting me as a writer and now a publisher is legion, and for that I am very grateful. Others, too, helped in the process: my three children, Sam, Emma, and Joe Carmichael, heard countless stories about composting and grew up listening to me expound on the merits of doing it—they are also incredibly supportive of my gardening, and writing. My mother, Shirley Ellis Cummings, wonderful editor and supportive parent and friend, was also a great source of inspiration and help.

Next, I'd like to thank the folks at Highfields. When I first called Kim Mercer, the director of communications, she was so supportive and wanted to help immediately. Another great connection at Highfields came from Maia Hansen, who also wanted to help make this book a reality. I am grateful to everyone there for the good work they did in Vermont to educate children, farmers, and regular people about the benefits of composting.

I received the same welcome from the folks at GROW NYC. From Amanda Gentile and Laura McDonald in the press corps, I received tremendous support; also one of the first people I spoke with was Christina Salvi, Assistant Director in the Office of Recycling Outreach and Education, who was incredibly helpful from the beginning. Everyone at GROWNYC is doing a terrific job! Go NYC: Show the world how it is done!

Karl Hammer at Vermont Compost Company was and is my new hero. I haven't met him yet, but love what he is doing, and on a national scale! Ron Finley, in Los Angeles, is another personal hero of mine . . . what a great thing he is doing with kids in the inner city!

My friend and Vermont neighbor, Vern Grubinger, was another supporter of this book. Vern is the extension professor and the vegetable and berry specialist at the University of Vermont. I am grateful for his help and support and his work to support organic farming and sustainable initiatives.

Lastly, the work of my editorial intern Cheyenne Vaughn was incredible! Cheyenne earned college credit from Bennington College while she researched and wrote sections of this book—she is an incredibly talented young woman and I am going to follow her career, fully expecting her to end up an editor at Skyhorse perhaps!

I am grateful, lastly, to all the composters out there! Whether you live in an apartment, a country home, or a dorm room, you *are* making a difference and I salute you all for living on the earth in a sustainable manner. Thanks to all!

PHOTO CREDITS

INDEX

Note: Sidebars are marked with a b after the page number.

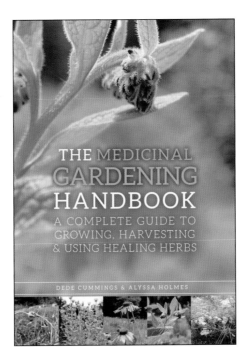

The Medicinal Gardening Handbook
A Complete Guide to Growing, Harvesting, and Using Healing Herbs

by Dede Cummings & Alyssa Holmes

Foreword by Barbara Fahs

Dig into the world of herbal medicine with this complete guide to cultivating and harvesting plants with healing properties. For thousands of years people have been utilizing herbs and cultivating weeds found to speed the healing of wounds, soothe skin irritations, calm uneasy stomachs, and ward off illnesses. Now you can plan and grow your own garden first-aid kit.

In these pages, you'll learn the basics of gardening in your backyard—or on your windowsill or porch—including instructions for preparing soil, composting, and weeding. You'll then find detailed descriptions of the twelve most common, easy-to-grow, most useful healing herbs, with instructions for growing, harvesting, and utilizing them. These powerful plants include:

- Garlic, which boosts immunity, reduces blood pressure, and combats cancer
- Echinacea, which reduces inflammation, boosts immunity, and has antiviral properties
- Yarrow, which accelerates the healing of wounds, is an anti-inflammatory, and can relieve PMS symptoms
- Elderflower, which is an astringent and can relieve arthritis and soothe sore throats
- Mint, which soothes digestive problems, sweetens breath, and can reduce fevers
- Elecampane, a respiratory tonic with antibacterial and antifungal properties
- And more!

$14.95 Paperback • ISBN 978-1-62914-195-4

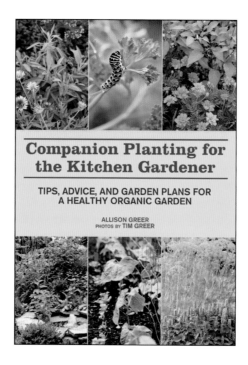

Companion Planting for the Kitchen Gardener
Tips, Advice, and Garden Plans for a Healthy Organic Garden

by Allison and Tim Greer

Companion planting techniques have been used for centuries to facilitate better, more nutritious, and more abundant crops. Did you know that beets will grow better if surrounded by mint or garlic, but tomatoes should not be planted near cabbage? Flax helps protect some root vegetables from pests, and tomatoes will thrive when planted near carrots (though the carrots may wind up stunted). Your celery will be happier if it's far away from corn, but broccoli and dill make a terrific garden pair. It's a lot to think about, but there's no reason to feel overwhelmed. With *Companion Planting for the Kitchen Gardener*, you'll have all the information you need in clear, concise terms and with charts and garden plans you can copy or modify to suit your family's needs.

Starting with the basics of organic gardening, such as how to prepare quality soil and the importance of cover crops and organic fertilizer, authors Allison and Tim Greer explain the principles of companion planting, how plants interact, and how you can use that information to your garden's benefit. There is an entire chapter devoted to each of the fifteen most popular vegetables, with charts, diagrams, and descriptions of each—a treasure for gardeners with busy lives who want an easy reference guide for planning their ideal kitchen garden. Full of gorgeous, full-color photographs and easy-to-follow diagrams, this is a beautiful, useful guide for the home organic gardener.

$14.95 Paperback • ISBN 978-1-62914-171-8

The Urban Garden

How One Community Turned Idle Land into a Garden City and
How You Can, Too

by Jeremy N. Smith

Fifteen people—plus a class of first graders—tell how local food, farms, and gardens changed their lives and their community . . . and how they can change yours, too.

The Urban Garden includes:

- Fifteen first-person stories of personal and civic transformation from a range of individuals, including farmers and community garden members, a low-income senior and troubled teen, a foodie, a food bank officer, and many more

- Seven in-depth "How It Works" sections on student farms, community gardens, community supported agriculture (CSA), community education, farm work therapy, community outreach, and more

- Detailed information on dozens of additional resources from relevant books and websites to government programs and national non-profit organizations

- Over eighty full-color photographs showing a diverse local food community at home, work, and play

Read *The Urban Garden* to:

- Learn how people like you, with busy lives like yours, can and do enjoy the many benefits of local food without having to become full-time organic farmers

- Gain the information you need to organize or get involved in your own "growing community" anywhere across the country and around the world

$24.95 Paperback • ISBN 978-1-62914-399-6

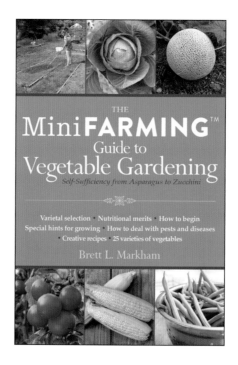

The Mini Farming Guide to Vegetable Gardening
Self-Sufficiency from Asparagus to Zucchini

by Brett L. Markham

Make the most of your vegetable garden with Brett Markham, author of *Mini Farming: Self-Sufficiency on Acre*. This comprehensive new handbook covers everything you need to know about maximizing and harvesting the best vegetables you can possibly produce. With each chapter addressing a different vegetable, you'll learn tips and tricks about varietal selection, nutritional merits, how to begin, special hints for growing, and how to deal with particular pests and diseases, plus one or two creative recipes to get you started. With over 150 of Markham's own photographs guiding you every step of the way, you'll find this an honest, straightforward guide and a must-have for any vegetable minifarmer.

$14.95 Paperback • ISBN 978-1-61608-615-2

NOTES

NOTES